Uncontrollable Societies of Disaffected Individuals

For my Écusette de Noireuil,[*]
in memory of Léonie and Frédéric Stiegler

Translator's note: See André Breton, *Mad Love* (Lincoln and London: University of Nebraska Press, 1987), p. 111, and the translator's note on p. 129: 'a double switch between the words *écureuil*, or squirrel, and *noisette*, or hazelnut'.

Uncontrollable Societies of Disaffected Individuals

Disbelief and Discredit, Volume 2

Bernard Stiegler

Translated by Daniel Ross

polity

First published in French as *Mécréance et Discrédit tome II: Les sociétés incontrôlables d'individus désaffectés* © Éditions Galilée 2006

This English edition © Polity Press, 2013

Polity Press
65 Bridge Street
Cambridge CB2 1UR, UK

Polity Press
350 Main Street
Malden, MA 02148, USA

ISBN-13: 978-0-7456-4811-8
ISBN-13: 978-0-7456-4812-5(pb)

A catalogue record for this book is available from the British Library.

Typeset in 11 on 13 pt Sabon
by Toppan Best-set Premedia Limited
Printed and bound in Great Britain by MPG Books Group Limited, Bodmin, Cornwall

The publisher has used its best endeavours to ensure that the URLs for external websites referred to in this book are correct and active at the time of going to press. However, the publisher has no responsibility for the websites and can make no guarantee that a site will remain live or that the content is or will remain appropriate.

Every effort has been made to trace all copyright holders, but if any have been inadvertently overlooked the publisher will be pleased to include any necessary credits in any subsequent reprint or edition.

For further information on Polity, visit our website: www.politybooks.com

Those aspirations were all the stronger because, with the coming of the Iron Age, the powerful lost all decency, and *Aidos* had to flee the world for the heavens. With the way thus left clear for the unleashing of individual passions and *hybris*, social relations were marked by violence, guile, despotism, and injustice.

Jean-Pierre Vernant, The Origins of Greek Thought

Fable has it that, in spite of the dress woven by the Graces, Venus was wounded by Diomedes. The vulnerability of the goddess is put in specific terms. Love, in what is most earthly about it – Venus endangered herself in order to defend Aeneas, the son she had from the most backward man, the shepherd – has to be touched during the course of life in its flesh, and the myth writer was careful to specify, in their ineluctable linking, the facts that are to bring about this passing mortification. At their origin Eris, or Discord, rages, engraving on the golden apple the fateful inscription: 'To the most beautiful'.

[...]

It is at the price of a wound required by the adversary powers who control man that living love triumphs.

André Breton, Mad Love

Contents

Introduction

In the summer of 2005 I prepared to write the second volume of *Disbelief and Discredit*, which, in *The Decadence of Industrial Democracies*, I indicated was to be subtitled *The Aristocracy to Come*. But as has happened to me before, my work programme was disrupted by events: the attacks carried out in London in July diverted me from my subject. Furthermore, progress was held up for several weeks owing to illness, and I was unable to complete the work before the end of summer.

Returning to Paris, I resumed my professional activities. Autumn was very hectic. Re-reading in December what I had written, just after the suicide bomber attacks in England, on Antigone and youth, on despair – what I call here spiritual misery [*misère spirituelle*]* – and on the reasons for hope, these words and phrases seemed in retrospect to foreshadow in a troubling way what occurred in France during November, following the tragedy of Clichy-sous-Bois in which two young men were electrocuted.

---

* *Translator's note*: Throughout this work the author refers, among other things, to *misère symbolique* and *misère spirituelle*, and these are mostly translated as 'symbolic misery' and 'spiritual misery'. This translation is generally preferred so that the reader can, so to speak, still hear the French in the translation, but it should be remembered that perhaps the more usual sense of *misère* is poverty or destitution, although, of course, Stiegler is playing on these meanings. On occasion 'immiseration' will be used, if it better suits the context.

Worse than that, these words and phrases seemed to echo in advance the terrible findings of the Beauvais court when it convicted Patricia and Emmanuel Cartier of murdering their own child.*

During these atrocious months, throughout which so much was said that only a few years earlier would have been virtually unimaginable, even during the 'colonial era', several short works were published about capitalism that warned of impending catastrophe, such as *Le capitalisme total*, by Jean Peyrelevade, and *Le capitalisme est en train de s'autodétruire*, by Patrick Artus and Marie-Paule Virard. These two works claim – as I myself argued in *The Decadence of Industrial Democracies*, though for different reasons – that the current socio-economic model of industrial production has become obsolete. This second volume of *Disbelief and Discredit* is thus also a sort of indirect dialogue with these works and their theses.

Symbolic misery leads irresistibly to *spiritual* misery. By this expression I refer firstly to that which paralyses the functions of the human spirit. The word *'esprit'*[†] refers here to a noetic process that is both psychic *and* collective (cerebral and social): spirit is what *exceeds* the *I* and connects it to the *we*, the condition of the *'and'* of psychic *and* collective individuation, just as is, moreover, technics. The spirit I am referring to is not some kind of vapour or pure idea, a pure form, or even what one calls 'pure spirit', but

---

* *Translator's note*: The riots and civil arrest that took place in France in November of 2005 were triggered by the deaths by electrocution of Zied Benna and Bouna Traoré in the Paris suburb of Clichy-sous-Bois on 27 October 2005. The teenagers had climbed into an electrical relay station and touched a high-voltage transformer, and many blamed their deaths on the police, sparking nearly three weeks of disturbance across France. For the Cartiers, see chapter 4 below.
† *Translator's note*: Esprit in French refers both to mind and spirit. At times one or other of these terms fits better, but mostly Stiegler's use of this term implies both these senses. It should be added that 'spirit' here, however, is not meant in any vaporously 'spiritual' sense, as he makes clear in the remainder of the paragraph.

that which, *passing through the organization of matter*, opens the process of conjunctions and disjunctions, and thus of trans-formations and trans-individuations, in which psychic and collective individuation *consists*.

And it is in this way – insofar as it is always already *both* psychic *and* collective – that knowledge [*connaissance*] is a fruit of spirit: knowledge exists only to the degree that it is *circulated and transmitted*, and to the degree that, through this transmission, it is trans-formed, engendering new knowledge(s) (thereby constituting the history of what Husserl called a 'transcendental we'), and therefore also as such forming and trans-forming the *course* of individuation at its highest level. Knowledge [*connaissance*] is, however, itself only a highly refined form of those types of knowing [*savoirs*] that constitute spirit. Now, the latter are, first and foremost – including in those societies that lack knowledge [*connaissance*] (understood here as theoretical formalization) – the knowledge of *savoir-faire* (know-how, skill) and *savoir-vivre* (knowledge of how to live).

The process of individuation today, and insofar as it consists in a permanent trans-formation of *savoir-faire*, of *savoir-vivre*, and of knowledge [*connaissance*], occurs only in *conditions of extreme control*, to the point that it becomes doubtful that this is still a matter of individuation. Gilbert Simondon expresses such doubt in relation to the *savoir-faire* of the worker-become-proletarian,[1] hence his assertion that the proletariat has been *disindividuated*. And I myself harbour such doubts in relation to the *savoir-vivre* of consumers, whom I believe to be disindividuated, and thus proletarianized in their turn, resulting in what I have called generalized proletarianization.[2] It is, in the end, questionable whether that knowledge engendered by the industrialization of knowledge and by cognitive technologies – in particular insofar as these produce a syndrome of *cognitive saturation*, and have *entropic* effects for hypotheses, axioms, and research methods – still *constitutes* a genuine process of individuation for the contemporary *épistémè*.

More particularly, spiritual misery, insofar as it is the blockage or destruction of psychic and social circuits through which the objects of spirit are constituted – which are the objects of *admiration*, *sublimation*, and *love* (of art, science, language, knowledge, and wisdom, which in Greek is called *philo-sophia*) – this blockage or this destruction, then, also engenders an *anxiogenic situation* that *aggravates and reinforces* this paralysis of the human psychosocial spirit: the noetic soul feels that, deprived of its premier faculty, thought, its capacity to discern and therefore to anticipate, and to *want and act knowingly*, is *radically threatened* – and with it, the human species in totality.

The noetic soul tends, then, to *regress towards reactive behaviour and the survival instinct*, which induces, in the desiring beings that we are, the *reign of the drives [pulsions]* – and in particular the drives of destruction and of those compulsions that are its symptoms, thus resulting in the proliferation of addictions. The spiritual functions are, then, wholly tetanized, resulting in a vicious circle that can lead, if it persists, only to *panic behaviour*. This adjective, 'panic', haunted by the god Pan and his Syrinx, refers here not merely to fear, but to the *herdish reactions* induced by this fear, in which *all* (in Greek, *pan*) are included. This is, then, the *reign or kingdom of stupidity [règne de la bêtise]*.

We live under this reign: such is our misery. Now, this situation engenders in its turn a new element of desublimation, that is, of de-spiritualization or, in Valéry's terms, of 'the lowering of the spirit value, *la valeur esprit*', if not its absolute destruction: *despair [désespoir]*, that is, the destruction of the *kingdom of ends* in which, as Kant taught, reason consists. Reason is in fact intrinsically tied to hope [*espoir*], or in other words to aims – even if only in the form of idealities and noemes, and those idealizations that Freud described as being intrinsically engendered by the amorous life in which the human spirit specifically consists – goals and motives without which the human being is little more than an algorithmic machine, that is, a system of comparisons reducible to a set of calculations without a point [*sans objet*].

What Weber called disenchantment bears within it such a becoming, a becoming reactive and, ultimately, stupid [*bête*], and this is also what Nietzsche referred to as nihilism. This becoming brings about the fall of those metaphysical delusions that philosophy itself undermined by elaborating, through the centuries, the *spirit of critique*, that is, of freedom. For this reason, however, this becoming brings with it the potential for an unprecedented transformation: it calls forth a *new epoch of the spirit, that is, of civilization*.

But more immediately, this results in the forms of spirit transmitted by this disenchantment process being destroyed *without being trans-formed*, that is, without leading to their *individuation*, and it is for this reason that I claimed, in the first volume of *Disbelief and Discredit*, that we are living through a *decadence* of industrial democracy.

Disenchantment, when carried to extremes, may have allowed capitalism to conquer the entire world, but it eventually leads to the *loss of the capitalist spirit*. Now I believe, as Weber undoubtedly believed, and as Luc Boltanski and Ève Chiapello believe,[3] that a capitalism totally deprived of spirit, that is, in the end, of motivation, or in other words of *motives for living*, of what I have just called the kingdom of ends – such a capitalism, *having lost its spirit or its mind*, is not possible. Unlike Boltanski and Chiapello, I do not believe that current capitalism has engendered a 'new spirit of capitalism'. I believe, on the contrary, that capitalism is very profoundly threatened *by itself*, and that this is the reason, whether consciously or otherwise, why MEDEF [Mouvement des Entreprises de France, the French business organization] took the 're-enchantment of the world' as the theme of its summer school in 2005, while in the meantime several books have appeared, some from the economic and financial spheres, that are critical of the direction in which contemporary capitalism is headed.

The destruction of spirit leads to the loss of all hope, but also to the loss of the very possibility of constituting horizons of expectation of a *we*. This is the result when capitalism – in order to penetrate every market and to exploit every possibility revealed by industrial innovation, at the same time continuously disrupting social structures, that is, those systems of collective individuation through which psychic individuals find their place – succeeds in destroying every barrier to the circulation of commodities. The circulation of commodities, then, comes to replace the circulation of the works of spirit, and as such leads to the outright *liquidation of the super-ego* as a system of prohibitions, and to the liquidation of *sublimation as that socialization through which desire constitutes itself insofar as, being psychic, it is always already also collective* – including in its transgressive forms, these being what I refer to as the Antigone complex.

This loss of spirit above all takes the form, massively, of industrial populism, the exploitation of 'available brain time', systematically targeting drive-based and regressive mechanisms, and operating *against spirit understood as the care taken of the objects and subjects of* individual and collective *desire* – including the *care taken of children*. As I have argued in *Constituer l'Europe 1. Dans un monde sans vergogne*, industrial populism leads to the destruction of all shame (*aidos*), that is, to the liquidation of all sublimation and all super-egoization: all *law* and, therefore, all *justice*. This populism, then, reigns, along with cynicism and a transgressive acting out that, animated by a pure death drive, fails to lead to any transindividuation, or to any possibility of sublimation – except in the frightening form that I call, notably in relation to the behaviour of terrorists, *negative sublimation* (of which Freud tentatively initiated an analysis).

The loss of the spirit of capitalism, and the spiritual misery to which it leads, can engender only the development of a society that is profoundly *irrational*, in the sense that reason has disappeared as the *motive of hope*, as the kingdom of ends. *Absolute* disenchantment is the *disappearance of every horizon of expectation*, and of all belief, whether religious, political, *or libidinal*, which is also to say filial and social, constituting as such that fabric of solidarities necessary for any society – which Aristotle named *philia*. This absolute disenchantment afflicts in particular all those who *no longer have anything to expect* from the development of hyper-industrial society – and such people are becoming *more and more numerous*.

Now, no longer having anything to expect also means no longer having anything to fear, something already indicated by the Greek word *elpis*: expectation, which bears within it the sense of both hope and fear. With desperation comes a lack of fear – and the proliferation of repressive mechanisms intended to cope with the effects of this *loss of authority that is also a loss of spirit* turns out to be less and less effective and, ultimately, to increasingly engender *the opposite* of that for which they were intended, in extreme and totally irrational forms. This is the point at which we have arrived, and it is *very* bad news: the *hyper-power* of the technical system of the hyper-industrial epoch can maintain its power only for as long as everyday, blind trust [*confiance*] remains possible, a trust inevitably ruined by the destructive irrationality resulting from the liquidation of the kingdom of ends. Now, trust is a *precondition* of the functioning of hyper-power: from the moment trust is lost, hyper-power is inverted into hyper-vulnerability and impotence. The loss of motives of hope, then, spreads, encompassing *all* of us like a contagious illness. But this '*all*' is no longer a *we*: it is a panic.

The loss of all expectation [*attente*] is, moreover, what in the first place engenders industrial populism, through the *destruction of attention itself*. Industrial populism exploits control technologies, and in the first place television, as Gilles Deleuze made clear during an exchange with Serge Daney. I try to show in this work that *the control of attention inevitably induces the uncontrollable* because it is above all the control of what Freud analysed as the processes of primary and secondary identification. It is through these processes that a psyche, that is, a psychic individuation, is constituted, a psychic individuation that, as a result of secondary identifications (themselves forming secondary retentions), is also a collective individuation. The process of primary identification – which was placed, even quite recently, under the authority of the parental *imago*, and, through the intermediary of parenthood, of revenances weaving a heritage of spirit, and as its spirits and hauntings – has to a large extent ceded control to the flux of industrial temporal objects and, in particular, those of television. Now, this situation ruinously overdetermines all those processes of secondary identification through which the psyche is woven – a ruin that results in the reign of spiritual misery.

Controlling primary and secondary identification leads to psychic dis-identification, which in turn leads to a process of collective disindividuation, that is, to a destruction of the social body itself, and engenders disaffected psychic and social individuals. It does so in a dual sense: it engenders their *disaffection* [*désaffection*], ruining their affective capacities; and it engenders their *withdrawal* [*désaffectation*], the loss of their place, that is, of their *ethos*. For this amounts to the question of ethics: ethics, which is the knowledge of the *abode* [*séjour*]. Ethics, as the translation of the Greek word *ethos*, is that which gives me my *place* within the *circuit of affects* through which the process of psychic and collective individuation constitutes itself. Insofar as it establishes such places, ethics is also what weaves that process of transmission linking together the succession of generations.

This book, which tries to think what the *place of youth* might be today, speaks of ethics, mores, and morality in the hyperindustrial epoch. It is a matter of thinking ethics, mores, and morality – that is, everything that forms what is also called the super-ego – in their original relation to justice and law. But this presupposes that justice and law are distinguishable: law is *the positive and finite existence* of that of which justice is the *consistence*; justice itself, then, is something that does not exist – given that, *like every object of desire*, it is infinite. Nevertheless, the relation of justice and ethics, on the one hand, and of justice and law, mores and morality, on the other hand, is itself over-determined by the becoming of technics [*technique*] and of its contemporary actuality, technology [*technologie*], such that it conditions, throughout the ages, the processes of individuation at the core of which are formed the *motives for living* that are justice and ethics, taken as principles.

The global technological and industrial system, which Dominique Janicaud analysed as the *power of the rational*, becomes the *impotence of the irrational* as soon as control societies become unliveable societies composed of disaffected individuals, that is, uncontrollable individuals. Such is the reality of the reversal of values to which nihilism leads. Irrational here means: leading to the loss of every motive for living, and to despair.

This gloomy development is the completion of desublimation, culminating in the outright liquidation of the super-ego. Here, desublimation takes the form not only of the liquidation of narcissism – that is, as psychic disindividuation, which I have analysed in my preceding works – but also of the destruction of that *collective desire* through which alone the super-ego can *consist*. Justice, which does not exist, and of which law, which does exist, is the super-egoic translation, is first of all that desire referred to as *philia*. And the destruction of *philia* inevitably leads to the reign of injustice, and thus also to the reign of stupidity, that is, barbarity.

The question of politics is thus that of justice insofar as, *as motive*, it is the *rationality* of the process of psychic and collective individuation, itself consisting in the process of the *unification of multiplicity*, psycho-social individuation being nothing other than this unification process, and rationality being a thinking that both operates by *critical argumentation* and *desires* its object, and that, as such, *maintains* desire for this object – by taking care of it. Conversely, the irrational engenders de-motivation, however 'rationalized' it may be through systems of calculation and control, systems that may nevertheless produce irrationality, that is, de-motivation. Justice can only *consist* as an object of desire: only in this way can it constitute its *authority*. Justice can never be reduced to that *repression* that is nevertheless *also* positive and finite law. Now, the liquidation of the super-ego causes societies to become police-societies, and, when this turns into the concrete expression of what Marcuse called the *automatization of the super-ego*, it destroys the desire for justice and leads to *psychic and social* conflicts of an extreme nature and violence: conflicts that promise a society-become-uncontrollable, that is, -unliveable.

Justice, a notion that first appears when society becomes political, is what constitutes the super-ego *while (and in) criticizing it*: as such, it is *transgression* as a *dynamic* of the Western individuation process, but a transgression that, as sublimation, is socialized in the form of a passage to the *noetic* act. Dis-identification, engendered by a symbolic misery that then becomes spiritual misery, *prevents* sublimation. It prevents acting out, this *passage to the act by* the noetic act, and engenders *regressive, drive-based, and suicidal* acts.

This leads to the installation of a system of terror, and this is what we must struggle against. For if what Simondon called transindividuation is the reality of sublimation and super-egoization, then today this has been short-circuited by marketing – and it was in such a context that Patricia and Emmanuel Cartier, intoxicated and poisoned by hyper-consumption, were able to commit their infanticidal crime. And it is in such a context that disruptive children [*enfants turbulents*], deprived of normal affective lives through media brainwashing [*le matraquage médiatique*], can be accused of suffering from 'behavioural problems', for which their parents can then be blamed. Blaming parents serves to mask, through a psychopathological discourse, the *sociopatho-logical* situation that in fact results from the reign of spiritual misery.

And this was the very basis on which Nicolas Sarkozy proposed a politics founded on a false interpretation of the spiritual as well as the religious (with which, wrongly, he confounds it), thereby sparing himself the necessity of criticizing the calamitous becom-ing of the culture industry, an industry that is one of the *main factors* leading to dis-identification, that is, to the ruin of all authority of the spirit and, with it, of the super-ego.

Contrary to what Peter Sloterdijk seems to believe, I do not think that humanity can be domesticated. I believe, on the contrary, that human beings ceaselessly oscillate between the *desire for taming* and the *temptation of fury*. By taming I mean that humans carry within them a savagery that they trans-form into singularity: this singularity is a potential for socialization, but such that it proceeds from what Kant called 'unsocial sociability'. This taming is pro-duced under conditions of what I call a process of adoption,[4] and such that this process is above all technical.

When Sophocles, in the first choral ode of *Antigone*, speaks of humankind as a disquieting, terrifying, monstrous, or marvellous being (*to deinotaton*), this is immediately related to humanity's technics, referred to by Sophocles as *mekhanoen tekhnas*, a tech-nics that 'exceeds all hope', that is, all *elpis*, thus also all *expecta-tion*, and that exceeds as such man himself, who must, in order to *tame* himself, begin by taming technics – a taming that, however, never constitutes a mastery. Humanity is, at bottom [*en son fond*], savage and furious, and this ground or fund [*fond*] is trans-formed into technical power, and is in this way socialized and tamed – but this tamed sociality must be made the object of a *care*. This care is what I call here spirit [*esprit*], which is also called, in Greek, *nous*. The human being is in this sense noetic, but its noeticity, that is, its spirituality, which is its power or potential, passes into actuality only (that is, is effective only) *intermittently* – as I tried to show in the final chapter of *The Decadence of Industrial Democracies*.

And this is why this adoption of technics by humankind, which is less about domesticating technics than it is about technics domesticating humanity itself, leads, in our epoch, to this misery or poverty that I call symbolic and ultimately spiritual, and eventually brings about what I have called, after William Burroughs and Gilles Deleuze, control societies: control societies exploit that tendency of noetic beings to regress to the level of the drives, to that level at which they become furious. How could it be, then, that control societies are not domesticating societies? How is it that this 'control' fails to make possible the *submission* of the human beast? The answer is that when human beings are controlled, and when this control deprives them of their desire, that is, their singularity, they become bestial and furious, in the sense that their drives are unleashed, until eventually they become radically uncontrollable.

Control societies, in other words, are not sustainable. If humanity is today subjected to a miserable symbolic condition, which places human beings into a situation of voluntary servitude where they are demeaned by the reign of stupidity, and in such a way that they also find themselves placed under control (not merely subjugated but nullified), and given that this kind of control is far worse than merely being under someone's command, then this symbolic poverty leads to a spiritual poverty that itself leads to the reign of destructive drives – to extreme social tensions, to the most varied and most disturbing transgressions [*passages à l'acte*], to terrorism, and tomorrow to war and perhaps, firstly, to civil war, that is, to the destruction of control societies themselves.

I completed this work in December 2005, in the course of a journey to Tokyo, during the final week of the year. *The Aristocracy to Come* will have to wait for another time: the urgency of events in the end led me to write two volumes: *Uncontrollable Societies of Disaffected Individuals* and *The Lost Spirit of Capitalism*. These volumes will show how *symbolic misery leads to a spiritual misery that passes into action*, and that this act is *criminal*.

As never before, I today fear the worst, shocked by the apathy of my contemporaries as much as by their fury. I find myself melancholic, angry, yet also ashamed of this melancholy, which has itself become so fashionable [*à la mode*], as if it had become our very mode of existence, or of inexistence, sometimes bland, yet always so profound and philosophical, and that fascinates us – and that kills us.

How could this intellectual and spiritual misery become the *very object* of philosophy without revealing itself as that *poverty of philosophy* [*misère de la philosophie*] the critique of which was so important to Marx? How to *nevertheless* practise a philosophy of misery, how to think a misery that critiques the poverty of philosophy without practising *miserabilism* – which is also to say, a sometimes subtle form of *populism*? This question, which demands a *sociology* of misery, but one orientated towards what I here name a sociopathology, calls for a discourse on the people and the popular, something I have outlined in another work dedicated to the theatre and written in collaboration with Jean-Christophe Bailly and Denis Guénoun.[5]

Be that as it may, speaking about misery always entails exposing oneself to the risk of becoming miserable, or impoverished, or destitute, in all kinds of ways: in the sense that one speaks of people without shame as being *misérables*, those who are the most in need of 'mercy' [*miséricorde*] (which is sometimes a *dagger*[6]), but also, miserable in the sense that it is only possible to speak of *that which affects the miserable* to the extent that one finds *oneself affected* in some way or other, to the degree that one *is* oneself such a 'miserable' – otherwise, it would not be possible even to imagine it. Now, this misery or poverty is a disaffection, and the problem is thus to think how a disaffection affects me, and in what way I am already, myself, such a disaffected individual.

In other words, it cannot be a matter of placing oneself outside of what is described here, which consists in further developing the general reflections I have previously conducted in relation to symbolic misery or poverty, through analyses or outlines of new forms of *economic* poverty, *psychological* poverty, *political* poverty, *intellectual* poverty, and the *spiritual* poverty to which these lead.

This work – which was, therefore, written to some extent as an echo of events that together form a system of symptoms – has become two works, the second and third volumes of *Disbelief and Discredit*. Volume 2 describes our fate, that is, uncontrollable societies and the disaffection and withdrawal of individuals, analysed in large part through the suffering of youth and of their ancestors [*ascendants*], and as the installation of a spiritual misery that I believe to be specific to our time. Volume 3* tries to turn back to the year 1968, on the one hand through a discourse on the role that it will have played in the fact that *capitalism has become a control society*, and on the other hand by re-reading Marcuse's major work, *Eros and Civilization*. It formulates hypotheses about the genesis of this spiritual misery that leads to uncontrollable societies, and outlines the idea of a *sociopathology*, a concept that Marcuse attempted to form – but on a largely erroneous Freudian basis, and for which 'May '68' was the confirmation of both its historic *sense* and its historic *error*.

---

* *Translator's note*: See Stiegler *Mécréance et Discrédit 3. L'esprit perdu du capitalisme* (Paris: Galilée, 2006), to be published by Polity as *The Lost Spirit of Capitalism*.

1

Despair and the Impotence of the Rational

And an unhealthy thirst
Darkens my veins.

> Arthur Rimbaud, 'Song of the Highest Tower'

Messenger: In this world, of all the misfortunes tied to man, stupidity is the greatest.

> Sophocles, *Antigone*

Here, there is no hope,
No orietur.

> Arthur Rimbaud, 'Eternity'

1. Impotence of the rational and the ruins of trust

In Morocco in the summer of 1987 I happened to need to drive from Temara, in the south of Rabat, to Casablanca. Abdelkebir Khatibi, director of the University Institute of Scientific Research, recommended that I avoid the ring road: at night, children in the shantytown that it crossed sometimes threw stones from a bridge onto windscreens. Some years later I heard reported on French radio that in Italy, on the coast of Naples, some children had caused spectacular accidents by throwing things onto vehicles travelling along the freeway and thus passing through their impoverished neighbourhoods. Broadcasting this news on Italian television had as its rapid consequence the mimetic migration of these acts to other Italian regions, to the point where police were forced to negotiate with the media to persuade them not to cover these incidents – copycat versions of which nevertheless reached as far as Orange, in France, several days later.

In an industrial democracy, the 'power of the rational'[1] is implemented everywhere and permanently in order to increase technical efficiency – by means of objects, apparatus, and machines that form a globally integrated and functionally integrated technical system. To live in the extremely complex milieus that deploy this industrial and planetary technical system, a system capable of unleashing colossal power at any instant, requires of the people traversing them that they maintain a blind trust. And this must be a blind trust not only in these machines, this apparatus, this infrastructure, and all those who maintain them, but also in all those other people who make use of the technical system and who behave more or less rationally. And, finally, it requires a blind trust in all those who are forced to 'live' within the system, and who, despite having to put up with all the problems and pollution it produces, are frequently unable to make use of the system or derive any benefit from it (unlike users of the system, such as, for example, motorists).

As the Third World extends further into the industrial world, this being so often the reality of globalization, there are increasing numbers of people who find themselves excluded from technological development, who benefit the least from such development, and yet who suffer the most from its many forms of pollution.

When we travel at high speed on the freeway, we trust spontaneously and unreflectively in the bridges and roadways of which the freeway is constructed, in the society that maintains it, in the car industry that built our vehicle, in everyone who is travelling directly ahead of us, in mechanics, in service stations, in the police, in the systems dedicated to creating a smooth flow of traffic, in the driver about to overtake us, and so on. Without this *spontaneity of trust*, such a system – the freeway system – could not function. Now, this system refers to other systems that presuppose investment in the same spontaneous trust: for example, the metallurgical system of car construction, the petrochemical system of fuel production, the chemico-pharmaceutical system that maintains the physical and mental health of motorists, and the media system that informs motorists and predisposes them to this or that mood, this or that reaction.

All our behaviour presupposes a prior, spontaneous trust in technics, and in the *coherence* of a system that is clearly not reducible to the sum of the parts of which it is constituted: it involves phenomena of great complexity, including other users, and it solicits the capacity of society to adjust, in terms of economy, law, education, individual and collective behaviour, physical and mental equilibrium, and so on, through continuous evolutions of the performance of technical systems, that is, of their power.

Now, such a prior, spontaneous trust is possible only if everyone who lives within the local technical system profits directly or indirectly from its power. I must, for example, be able to trust, night and day, those pedestrians who stand on the bridge overhanging the freeway along which I drive, even if such pedestrians happen to be economically deprived of all the comforts of the car, and even if they are nevertheless forced to suffer, constantly, all the forms of pollution it causes. The cohesion of the global system that forms society in general and technics in general presupposes that those who do not own cars do not disrupt highway traffic through behaviour capable at any moment of rendering impotent a technological system that can be considered rational only so long as it works – *which presupposes that the beneficiaries of the system trust the system*. But this trust is itself possible only in a sustainable way, and it can thus work only in a sustainable way, if, for example, the car industry or the road construction industry supplies work and wages enabling those who inhabit these technical milieus to live in decent housing,[2] even if such a habitat is exposed to the pollutions of the system that supplies these resources to those who suffer within it. It is indeed true that the vulnerability of the technical system increases proportionally to its sophistication – and, for this reason, the price paid for the hyper-power of the current system is its hyper-vulnerability: this is the source of the increasing *uncontrollability* of control societies in the hyper-industrial epoch.

By failing to give to everyone, and in principle, reasons to live and to hope *in this world* for something better to come, trust will before long be ruined and the system will cease to function, and will no longer, therefore, supply anything to anyone – not even to those oligarchs who today more than ever use and abuse a power that destroys all reasons for hope, a power that is therefore *irrational*. The leading economist Patrick Artus no longer hesitates to write that 'capitalism is in the course of self-destructing'.[3] The riots that flared on the outskirts of French cities in December 2005 were an effect of having to suffer this irrationality – a very dangerous effect, if also very predictable, and, unfortunately, only the precursor to other, even more serious events that will inevitably occur if nothing is done to affirm and implement a new political and economic rationality in France, in Europe, and throughout the entire capitalist and industrial world. This work is dedicated to thinking the crucial elements of such a rationality.

2.   The irrationality of hyper-power and the rationality of justice: the vicious circle

A prior, spontaneous trust in the power of technological systems – such systems having become hyper-powerful, particularly after the development of digital technologies and telecommunications – which is the condition of trust of consumers, as well as financial markets, and therefore investors, is possible and conceivable only to the extent that *everyone* has an interest in the continuation of the functioning and development of the system, even those for whom it does not yield any immediate profit. *We must all have a reason to expect something from the functioning and development of the system*, and this reason to *expect* something can only be the expectation of a better future.

Only such a system is truly rational. Taking into account that the intrinsic vulnerability of a system will only intensify as it becomes increasingly complex, the development of a technological system that manifestly operates against society or against a part of society becomes *structurally irrational*. And such a system, in some industrial and mechanical way, inevitably produces unreason, madness [*déraison*] – either on the part of those who adopt behaviour that eventually seriously interferes with its functioning, or on the part of those who lose trust in a system from which they may nevertheless profit directly or indirectly, however small the profit may in fact turn out to be. I have called this second form of unreason, to which I shall return, de-motivation.[4] These two forms of unreason feed on each other and thus constitute, from the moment they are unleashed, a *vicious circle* – a vicious circle entailing, in the end, and inevitably, the destruction of the system itself.

The possibility that the system of hyper-power could be destroyed (a system that, insofar as it is hyper-powerful, is also hyper-vulnerable), the possibility that industrial civilization could be brought to absolute ruin merely by demonstrating its *innumerable vulnerabilities, vulnerabilities that become patent from the moment the system no longer harbours any reasons for hope* – this is what terrorism counts on. And this is especially the case for those desperados who no longer fear death, given that they inflict it upon themselves, and who are called, depending on which 'camp' one belongs to, either suicide bombers or martyrs. Such people are *intrinsically* invulnerable and uncontrollable, and no F16, no weapon (whether nuclear, chemical, biological, or psychological), no torture, no association between the CIA and other secret services (from Vladimir Putin to Mossad to the French DST and Intelligence Service) can prevent them. They will inevitably win their wars if a new economic and political rationality is not very quickly affirmed as the programme to come from a renaissance of industrial civilization, in France, in Europe, in the industrial world in general and, finally, at the level of the entire world and of its highest international bodies.

Now, technical rationality presupposes a *social* rationality that is called *justice*. Justice (*dikè*), with shame (*aidos*), from which it is inseparable,[5] is a name for the way in which human beings, insofar as they are constitutively technical beings,[6] can and must desire to live together. This being-together can be bound and maintained only through *philia*,[7] that is, through an affective relation of esteem, respect, friendship, familiarity, and – speaking here the language both of Freud and of a long Christian tradition (however distinct *philia* may be, in terms of its original motives, from *agapè*, that is, from *caritas*) – *love* in all its diverse forms, the energetic basis of which is the libido as the binding of the drives, and as the *exceeding of that drive-based stage* which animates all living things endowed with a nervous system (the latter constituting its reflex system), those drives that are also referred to as the 'instincts'. And it is only because the *drives become desire* to the precise degree that life becomes technical[8] that Zeus can send Hermes to bring the sentiments of *dikè* and *aidos* to mortals *after* the fault of Epimetheus and the flight of Prometheus, following which these mortals become technicians.[9]

3. Justice and desire

There is never actual justice [*La justice n'est jamais effective*]: injustice has always reigned everywhere, and will always reign. This is so because mortals live in *eris* (the ancient Greek word for competition [*émulation*]), where the worst is always already produced within the best (because *eris* can also become discord):[10] mortality is *ptosis* (decline, decomposition), that is, *the ineluctable tendency to regress*[11] and, as such, to lack the feelings of *dikè* and *aidos* – insofar as they are feelings for what is lacking or defective [*fait défaut(s)*]. This is the meaning of the 'saying' of Anaximander.[12] This is why such feelings – insofar as they are intrinsically deficient, even though they are constitutive, and are, in other words, the originary condition of mortality – must be *cultivated*.

As I have already recalled by way of a quotation from Heraclitus, there is a feeling for justice only because there is a feeling of injustice.[13] And this *distinction* between the just and the unjust can arise only for a life lived in *eris*, that struggle which is as much the condition of elevation and emulation as it is of the decline of those who destroy one another. This is why this struggle for elevation is in the first place the struggle for education.[14]

Dikè arises after mortals have formed themselves into technical beings – always exposed to the risk of discord (of bad *eris*, which is injustice, *adikias*) through the fact of their technicity, which is also their facticity, their being-without-quality, their (de)fault of essence and of origin, their being-by-default, of which the consequence is their being-only-intermittently [*n'être-que-par-intermittences*],[15] *being* signifying here *passing into action* [*passer à l'acte*]. If *dikè* thus arises after the advent of *tekhnè* as mode of life (of a life that is an existence, and that goes *beyond* mere subsistence), this justice, which does not in fact exist, must be what *animates* the global process. It must be what *moves* it precisely as its law insofar as this is its motive, and the motive of *eris* precisely insofar as it is *good eris*: as that right that the system of *power* [*puissance*] – which is *technical* life, through which the psychic and collective individuation process forms – must affirm, insofar as it passes from *potential to action* [*de la puissance à l'acte*], that is, to the fulfilment of individuation *as elevation*, and it must affirm this right precisely as that which is distinguished from fact. The system of power must affirm the necessity of the right, and it is precisely for this reason that it is distinguished from fact. It must be affirmed as the *very motive of individuation*, as the *reason* for individuation, which can only be a reason *to hope* – and to hope for the unhoped-for, *anelpiston*, or, in other words, to expect the unexpected[16] (whereas the distinction between right and fact is what the contemporary general expansion of the law of contracts tends to efface under the influence of the Anglo-Saxon business world and of the international organizations that it engulfs).

This reason for hope that is justice is the *protention* of individuation, insofar as individuation carries out (overall, globally, which is also to say, as civilization) the elevation of that technical life that one still calls ex-sistence. Justice is that protention arising from the retention in which individuation consists (as its preindividual milieu) as its future [*avenir*], which is also its 'advent' [*advenir*]. It is, in other words, the *time* of individuation – the fact that individuation is a temporalization. And that means, equally, that it is the faculty of imagination: that which is able to *bring about what has not happened*, and that projects the object of desire onto the real, as that possibility that is realized in the form of the new.

Justice *that does not exist* is as such *this right and this duty* that psycho-social individuation *projects* as the organization of its very future, insofar as its future can only be its *desire* for a future. Justice must be contained in the overall system (the technical, psychic, social, biological, and geophysical system) as the very energy of the system, that is, *as its very desire*. Justice, in other words, is the *fruit* of the libidinal economy par excellence – the *succulence* of the future ('My hunger feasting on no fruits here / Finds in their learned lack an equal savour'[17]). And this means that the destruction of this libidinal economy can only ruin justice and law.

4. Law and guilt: the marriage of Stupidity and Resentment

Justice *and* the law: we must distinguish between that justice that is intrinsically deficient because it does not exist, has never existed, and will never exist, and that justice that is necessary, that exists positively in the form of positive law, which is what justice that does not exist precisely lacks. Call *justice* that which juridically *consists*,[18] and *law* that which juridically *exists*. (As for customary law, it does not *thetically* experience this abyss between justice that consists and justice that exists, insofar as it does not *pose* their difference positively [*thesis*], that is, as that which institutes [*tithemi*]. This is why it has no jurisprudence. But this does not mean that it would be immutable: its application is often also its re-creation. There are clearly *customary* forms of individuation.)

If we must distinguish justice and law, what Antigone calls divine law and human law, then we must, in some way, while distinguishing them, make these two laws project into each other, in such a way that justice *is what must* present itself as the very *necessity* of that justice *that is lacking*, and of that *lack* in which, precisely, it consists (in being-only-intermittently). This is precisely Antigone's accusation against Creon: that he renounces this *composition* of consistence *into* existence, and of existence *through* consistence.

This projection, which can only be asymptotic, that is, a projection *to the infinite*, is what makes justice the very object of desire, insofar as objects of desire can only be infinite singularities, that is, incomparable [*sans commune mesure*], literally incommensurable (such is Antigone's love for Polynices) – and such objects, being incomparable, are not existent: they do not exist anywhere other than *in the desire* of which they are the object, while desire is that which can be extinguished or reignited only within the *phantasia* of a *psyche* populated by chimeras.

Certainly, that justice that does not exist is confronted every day by the existence of the *apparatuses of justice*, which are also the institutions of what Freud called the 'super-ego'. The super-ego is defined as that which *represses* the expression of desire – desire understood as *psychic energy*, but also, because the

psychic individuation process is immediately a collective individuation process, as *social energy*.

As super-ego, the process of psycho-social individuation tends
to *hypo-stasize* justice into law, in positing this as the *principle* of
its functioning.[19] A principle (*arkhè*) is only the principle of that
which *is* and *becomes*, and which, in this becoming, is nevertheless
maintained in its being, insofar as this principle is as such the
metastabilization of the process of which it is the principle. The
principle *connects* the past of this being-in-becoming (and which it
poses as its origin) to its future, of which it makes a destiny, a
binding that forms the *unity* of this becoming precisely as its *being*
(a bond that, when the Roman world is Christianized, takes the
form of that religion and canonical law, that is, divine law, con-
forming to the essence of the *summum ens* that is God). But this
unity that is, *as justice*, the *metastabilization* of a *motive* becomes,
as *law*, that which tends to *define* itself rather than infinitize itself:
it is then what tends to hypostasize itself as *identity*, in other words
as stability – and not merely as metastable unity – and therefore to
deny that it is a *process*. The principle of identity is thus what
superimposes itself in the play of the One and the Many: such is
the passage from the Presocratic age to Platonic metaphysics.[20]

In other words, the process tends to ontologize itself on the
basis of the *authority of an ancient principle* (of the archaic), that
is, also, of the *father*, who is thus *eternalized*. The super-ego, then,
becomes repressive in the strict sense, and tends to deny desire, to
prevent its expression by organizing itself as *censorship*. This
evolution is concretized in monotheism. And this, in various historical guises, is then imposed as the reign of guilt. And this is in
turn transformed, in the epoch of Nietzsche and Freud, but even
more so today, into the reign of Resentment [*Ressentiment*],
wedded to stupidity [*Bêtise*]. We will turn again to these questions
in the third volume.

5. Disindividuation in control societies as the liquidation of the super-ego and the reign of stupidity

In the most advanced forms of the hyper-industrial epoch of
control societies, super-egoization is liquidated, as is the figure
of the father, along with the authority of every principle. These

liquidations literally unleash *ressentiment* – hence certain cartoon-ish reactions that have recently appeared in France[21] – which, through a paradox that is only now becoming clear, and con-fronted with shameless transgressions [*passages à l'acte sans ver-gogne*], that is, with regressions towards the worst, transgressions and regressions that are ever more numerous, and ever worsen-ing, *tends to aggravate the process of culpabilization by increasing the spread of shamelessness.*

Censorship then becomes, at the same time:

- *self-censorship* and the social organization of inhibition through psychic as well as social *disindividuation*;
- the liquidation of barriers to the circulation and consumption of commodities, barriers that are singularities, and which are therefore censored;
- the consequent destruction of the primordial narcissism of the *I* and the *we*;
- the herdish growth of the *they* – the growth of this 'desert' that is the vile [*immonde*].

I argued in *The Decadence of Industrial Democracies* that what I call 'generalized proletarianization' engenders psychic disindi-viduation, and does so by particularizing singularities. What I am trying to show in this volume is that this process leads not only to problems of narcissism but also to problems for the super-ego, thus to a process of *collective* disindividuation, that is, to the liquidation of the social as such: to barbarism.

Disindividuation as the calculated particularization of singu-larities inevitably becomes the functional organization of the liberation of the drives in the service of consumption: if the exploitation of libidinal energy ruins it, then there is no longer any desire strictly speaking, *nor, therefore, any super-ego.* And since it remains necessary to continue selling the objects of industrial production, and since an exhausted libidinal energy can no longer fix onto these objects, the functional system that organizes the dispersal and sale of the flow of commodities, consciousness, and moods of all kinds, namely, the culture indus-try, incites what remains when all desire is gone – namely, the drives.[22]

Desire is nothing other than the *binding* of the drives and, when desire is liquidated, it is the drives that rule. In this reign, desire can no longer accomplish what is its essence, *sublimation*, through which psychic and social bodies are elevated as the *transindividuation* of individuations (as that process through which psychic individuation *concretizes* itself as *collective* individuation, which notably engenders all the collective secondary retentions through which symbols, meanings, and synchronic supports are constituted, all those elements through which is composed the diachronization in which individuation consists, and which confers on meanings their sense, that is, their motive: their *reason*).[23]

This is why the reign of the drives is also necessarily that of stupidity – *the worst of all evils*, as Sophocles said.

The worst of all evils, that is, the most *intimate*. Stupidity *inspires* shame: to experience stupidity as stupidity, to find oneself confronted by innumerable forms of stupidity, is to experience the shame of being human – that shame that the Greeks called *aidos* – the shame of being a mortal. The risk is, then, of treating stupidity as an error, or as the guilt of living this shame as a shame prior to guilt: the risk is of transforming one's own shame into guilt. This shame, which affects what is confronted in stupidity, is the experience of that stupidity that most intimately threatens what it affects as the possibility of one's *own* stupidity. And it is this structure of auto-affection that, then, tends to transform itself into guilt, that is, into *ressentiment* and denial. It is for this reason that Dork Zabunyan can write: '[F]rom a transcendental perspective, stupidity must therefore be understood as being *my own stupidity*, to the extent that my thought discovers itself as a truly engendered faculty (that is, in Deleuzian terminology, as a superior faculty) through this natural "powerlessness" that stupidity reveals to him in law.'[24]

6. Ethics and morality

If the liquidation of desire, to which the destruction of the libidinal economy in the hyper-industrial epoch of control societies leads, is also necessarily the liquidation of justice and law, that is, of the super-ego, then it is also that of *ethics*, of which *aidos* is the *knowledge*, the *savoir* (as succulence – savour – of that which is lacking and faulty [*fait défaut(s)*], that is, singularities). And this knowledge, as knowledge of that which is lacking, is also necessarily a non-knowledge, a knowledge that remains always to come, and towards which we must raise ourselves *insofar as it is that which consists without existing*.

This is why ethics is not morality: it is what, as shame, assigns to those susceptible to justice, to the justiciable, their place (their *ethos*), precisely insofar as they are subject to the difference between existence and consistence, which is also to say, to the experience of shame, to the intimacy of stupidity – insofar as they are neither of the gods, who purely and simply consist (*dikè* is first of all Dike, a goddess, and specifically the goddess to whom Hesiod addresses himself in *Works and Days*), nor of beasts, which merely subsist. Ethics, like justice, is what must be interpreted, and can thus never be codified. This is why it is Hermes, who is both the god of *hermeneia* and the god of writing (of *hypomnemata*), who brings these two feelings to mortals.

Ethics becomes morality when, as a law posing itself as an immutable principle, rather than as a process and object of individuation, that is, of desire, it rigidifies into a body of rules defined as *norms* of life, founded on guilt and thus denying the singularity of existences in their own experiences of the irreducible difference between that which exists and that which consists – which is also to say, denying the singularity of the *ethical interpretations* that are *concretized individuations*. But ethics as something held in common is also what is concretized as mores (*Sittlichkeit*).

In the age of morality and guilt, the lack of existence of that which consists is experienced as the fault of that which exists.

But this denial of the singularity of existence by morality is still not that disindividuation that organizes the reign of the drives in control societies. On the contrary, it constitutes a tendency to repression with which desire composes, and from which it nourishes itself, just as the reality principle is the *condition*, in every sense of the term, of the pleasure principle (this is what Jacques Derrida called their *stricture*).[25]

26   *Despair and the Impotence of the Rational*

7. Composition and decomposition (*ptosis*: decline, disbanding) of the libidinal economy: the reign of cynicism

The libidinal economy is an economy of tendencies, and the hypostatic temptation is always to assert either the primacy of one tendency or the primacy of the contrary tendency. The movement of desire, as process of individuation, does not cease composing with these two tendencies. By contrast, the disindividuation in which generalized proletarianization consists (the loss of both the *savoir-faire* and *savoir-vivre* of producers and consumers, which, depriving them of their possibilities of ex-sisting,[26] also deprives them of those elementary knowledge(s) that are *dikè* and *aidos*, and that constitute *the ethics and the justice of primordial narcissism*), produced by the hyper-synchronization of the times of consciousness (of 'available brain time') and of bodily movements (of behaviour, whether of production or consumption), induces the decomposition of these tendencies.[27] It is such a decomposition (*ptosis*) that enables disbelief and discredit to reign along with the drives: *the pure drive is purely cynical.*

Admittedly, the great shock that occurred in many countries in the spring of 1968 was to a large extent the result of a critique of morality and bourgeois law. It can be reasonably argued that it was Herbert Marcuse who inspired the youth of the entire world, and especially American youth, to this 'protest' movement (which was, however, also provoked by the cynicism of American politics in relation to the Vietnam war). For this is indeed how it came to be described – as a 'protest' – this critique that so suddenly and rapidly lost all critical spirit.

This ideology, calling for liberation from the social structures of the past (structures that had in fact rigidified, and that therefore did in fact require critique), spread after 1968 to every level of society and into every industrialized nation. There is no doubt that the expansion of this ideology slowly but surely led to the liquidation of state structures, and, beyond that, *to the simultaneous renunciation of public politics inspired by political belief, and to the 'flexibilization' of all social structures, leading them to eventually become those adjustable societies that are 'control societies', in which all existence and all consistence are reduced to the imperative to produce and circulate subsistences*. In other words, the reaction against governmental cynicism, of which the Vietnam war was a global symbol, a cynicism that emerged from reason, morality, and 'bourgeois' law, *this* reaction against cynicism that became the 'protest' itself *prepared the way for the advent of the unprecedented cynicism that characterizes the decadence of the industrial democracies* as the scourge of our age.[28]

All this ultimately leads, today, to an immense process of de-sublimation, that is, to the liquidation of ethics and justice – on which ever more claims are made. And it is at the moment they are liquidated that a 'return' to the 'values' of morality and law is most loudly trumpeted. But such values, without ethics and without justice, are without value. They make individuation impossible, and become purely repressive and profoundly regressive: they transindividuate nothing.

And this is what citizens know, and it is what they cannot believe. But by not believing, they become disbelievers and miscreants, that is, cynics. And thus is formed the vicious circle that will lead, if nothing changes, to a generalized politics of terror.

8. Justice and political economy

The entire difficulty of these questions – concerning the way in which desire and the super-ego must compose, and concerning these political principles that are justice and shame, *dikè* and *aidos*, which together form the conditions of all constitution and which are solely objects of desire (consistences), and which tend to rigidify into law and morality – lies in the fact that a process of individuation cannot avoid the tendency to hypostasize its *motive* in the form of a *principle* that represses desire. For this reason, there is no way that the struggle *against* this hypostasis can lead to a 'liberation of instincts',[29] except, precisely, by liquidating desire, and substituting for it the drives.

Whatever ambiguity there may be surrounding the principle that metastabilizes the process – and through which it risks rigidification, and inevitably tends towards this rigidification – a principle of binding (which is also a principle of reason[30]) is nevertheless what *must* affirm a *politics* insofar as it enunciates laws the unity of which can be constituted only as what is called 'the law', which is not justice, since such a law must be capable of being implemented as the very existence of a people, as that which actually exists or exists effectively, whereas justice could only be the consistence of such existences.

But a politics thus conceived as the ensemble of positive laws, and positively defined by this very politics, must also be a process of individuation that *desires* justice beyond the law[31] – and it must be so to the strict degree that it is nothing but the translation of *relations* between psychic individuals at the heart of a collective individual, configuring those *relations* [*rapports*] of which the basic conditions are *economic*: this political process is also an economic process, and the only way to have a principle of political binding is as *political economy*. Today, the conditions of political economy are industrial and technological. But industrial organization has come to contradict all forms of individuation, that is, libidinal economy, seriously impacting upon the social body from the side of the economy of subsistences (it impoverishes and even pauperizes the majority of psychic and social individuals).

Contrary to the politics of terror, the question is therefore that of politically asserting the *juridical necessity of a new industrial organization*, at a national as well as the European level, and finally the global level (as the *principle* of an international European politics).

Simondon poses with reason and as his *point of departure* that the *process* of individuation does not presuppose any *principle* of individuation – the process being on the contrary what already contains within it the obsolescence of every principle, that is, its passing, *intermittent*, or historical character. Even so, a political principle of binding – which can take diverse historical forms, or even regress to a proto-historical stage (such as that of the great Mesopotamian, Egyptian, or Chinese empires) – must metastabilize *as an epoch* (as a *doubly epochal redoubling*)[32] the functioning of the overall system that constitutes the process of individuation, and it must do so in such a way that the individuations of the technical system, the psychic system, and the social system co-individuate and are articulated with the vital system and the geophysical system. The principle that metastablizes the individuation of the technical system must cohere with the principle that metastabilizes the psycho-social system in which consists the development of those social and psychic systems that are human individuals and the groups they form, which must themselves be compatible with the vital and geophysical characteristics of the milieus they inhabit.

In other words, *such a political principle must today explicitly express a politics of technics* in the age of industrial technology, and it must therefore *put forward an industrial politics guided by the imperative of guaranteeing this coherence that is the condition of pursuing individuation*, that is, of the transindividuating expression of desire, of the projection of a *common desire* that is a *belief* in the future of the entire process: a belief in *justice*.

The coherence of the development of the three strands of individuation – the psychic, social, and technical strands, which co-individuate themselves and can be transformed only jointly, in transductive relation – can be constituted only through the *rationality of a belief* in the necessity of justice (in *what does not exist* and will *never* exist) as a horizon projected and *desired* by all, *each in his or her own way*, in a way compatible with the limits of *natural milieus* and *living beings*, and as the anticipation and realization of a *best* (*ariston*) that can (as we shall see) present itself only as the very figure of singularity.

This is why a politics of industrial technology capable of promising a future, which could be a politics only of the *culture* of singularities as the expression of the best, must be named an *aristocracy* – obviously in a re-elaborated sense of this ancient word, to which I shall return in the fourth volume of *Disbelief and Discredit*.

2

The Antigone Complex

Antigone: I am made to share love, not hate.

Sophocles, Antigone

1. Politics as critique of the super-ego and as sublime form of transgression

A society without authority, that is, without super-ego, is inconceivable. The point is not to *destroy* the super-ego – which would be to destroy society – but rather to *critique* the super-ego, and to make this a critique in the Kantian sense: to critique that which one cannot do without (as was the case, for Kant, with reason).

The *political* age – as the epoch of the psychic, collective, and technical individuation process that characterizes ex-sistence, that is, the way of life proper to those who are called human beings, and as the typically Western epoch of this process – is the age that has *instituted*, according to rules that vary in different times (depending on the political principles that are operating), the critique of the super-ego, that is, of *authority*. Political authority thus rests on its own critique, and this constitutes its discernment, that is, its *intelligence* as the political mode of transindividuation, and which designates itself as *logos* – insofar as this is distinguished from *muthos*, with which, however, it composes (which means that it does not oppose it, contrary to what is believed by fundamentalists of the *res publica*). This is why political authority is the authority of a judgement founding a legality that itself emerges from its own critique, that is, from its *auto-transgression*.

For the *citizen* is, then, the one qualified and authorized to judge, to decide, and as such the one in whom existence resides, not only by right but in the *duty* to critique the super-ego: to become the *interpreter* of, and if necessary to *contest*, the law, in the first place within the framework of jurisprudence and the trial, and then in those representative authorities that are the *Prytanies* and the *Boule*, in the *Prytaneion* and the *Bouleterion*, and in the Agora. This critique is made possible only by a *krinein*, a capacity to judge (*to krinon*), a discernment of which the laws themselves form the framework as the heritage of past judgements (including those laws that constitute the disciplines in general as *épistémè*), but of which the exercise presupposes an hypomnesic practice: a *skholè* (or in Latin, an *otium*).

Thus understood, the *skholè* is not simply of the order of sublimation, even if it is clearly related: *as* sublimation, it is, however, also and *above all*, insofar as it is critique, of the order of *transgression*. But the transgression involved here is in some way legal: a sublime acting out that expresses a desire – the desire for justice that wants the *boule*, which means, precisely, the will of the *demos* insofar as it is entitled and qualified to critique the super-ego.

Politics, in other words, at least in its initial idea, is the organization of a sublime form of transgression – which is also an original process of psychic, social, and technical individuation. And it is only through politics that other sublime forms of transgression can arise, such as, for example, scientific discoveries and epistemological ruptures. Before politics, other sublime forms of transgression existed: those lying at the origin of art, and which, like all *tekhnè* in general, were considered to be magical. The fact that the Presocratic thinkers were also poets, and were at times considered to be 'masters of truth', stems from the fact that they were themselves founders of cities and initiators of that new form of psycho-social and technical individuation that was the political relation. They made the link with the most ancient sublime forms of transgression – those that derive from magical worlds and from divination.

2.   Archaic or critical: youth, *hypomnesis*, and the authority of the best in the republic

When the political form reaches maturity, a conflict arises between, on the one hand, the *gerontocracy* (product of traditional society and based on the 'inherited conglomerate),'[1] and, on the other hand, Athenian *youth* (whom Socrates is accused by Anytas of corrupting). This conflict expresses a struggle between two models of authority. One derives from the *archaic* authority inherited from mythical figures and from the myths of the Greek divinities, especially Zeus, *father of the gods*, insofar as it is he who possesses *fire*. The other proceeds from the *critical* authority formed by the passage from *muthos* to *logos*.

But at the same time, this passage from *muthos* to *logos* takes place through *tekhnè*, this being both that which is possessed by Zeus, fire (the exploitation of which he delegates to Hephaestus), and that which constitutes mortals as beings-in-default – and which thus founds this mortality as *critical situation*, in all senses of the expression: perilous, having to decide, before judging and discerning in the elaboration of decisions. The technicity of mortals, deriving from the *theft of that power* that had been conferred on the father of the gods by fire, is their mortality as that temporality that arises through the process of their individuation *in the conditions* of this *tekhnè*. Now, the passage from *tekhnè* in general to *hypomnesis*, insofar as it is a specific form of *tekhnè*, is at the same time the condition of the passage from the mythological age to the logical age (the appearance of writing), and what the mythological age itself (which forms in the eighth century even as it begins to disappear, with advances in the practice of *hypomnemata*) foreshadows in the mythology of those complex figures that are Prometheus, Epimetheus, Hermes, Pandora, Athena, and Hephaestus – the *binding god*, as highlighted by André Green, following the work of Marie Delcourt.[2]

It is Hermes who brings the feelings of *dikè* and *aidos* to mortals, to the strict degree that he is the god of writing, that is, of *hypomnemata*, and as such of an interpretation that is no longer simply divination: when *dikè* and *aidos* become common nouns (just as *dikè* is derived from the goddess Dike, so too the word *aidos* without doubt derives from the name of a god, Hades, who reigns over the dead), they lose their divine status and become the very conditions of political constitution, and as such bring about a specifically Greek psycho-social individuation. But as former divinities, they are on another plane, and constitute as such *consistences which do not exist*.

Hermes delivers to mortals these notions now common to all mortals, and does so to the extent that consistences in general, and the consistence of *dikè* and *aidos* in particular, are only made *accessible to the judgement of citizens* through the *practice* of *hypomnesis* – which is the basis of law, and which is *public* law only insofar as it is *written* law, which one must *learn* to interpret. Through this they accede to these *new pre-individual funds* constituted by the inherited conglomerate, but also, in addition to ancient myths of authority, the new discourse of jurists, geometers, physiologists, Presocratic poets, the first historians, the first geographers, the first grammarians, and the first rhetoricians, all these being engrammed in the form of those particular tertiary retentions that constitute the orthography transmitted by the *grammatist*, master of letters, teacher of ortho-graphic order to the greedy (and idle) Athenian youth. In other words, the *krinein*, without which there would be no citizenry, also presupposes this practice of *hypomnemata* in *all* those domains that the appearance of *hypomnesis* made possible, which will be thematized by the Stoics and Epicureans as the *writing of oneself* through the practice of *tekhnè tou biou*.[3]

It is only through knowledge of ortho-graphy, instituted within the souls of the young, that citizens constitute themselves: they are *instituted* citizens only to the extent that they are *constituted* as literate and scholarly. It is only insofar as they are literate, it is only insofar as they have access to the *skholè*, and, through that, to consistences that do not exist (such as the geometric point[4]), that they can accede to what Plato called the idea – and above all to ideas of justice and shame – and, as such, to individuate the law through their capacity to interpret *dikè* and *aidos* through the interpretation of law itself, interpretation always having some relation to transgression.

The law should not, however, be confused with these ideas of what does not exist. For insofar as it is *positive* law, it also exists positively in the sense that it is inscribed on the stelae of public places and places of worship, bringing it to the attention of this public that forms the public space of the city insofar as it is a support of writing. And, as such, it constitutes – *through its very materiality, but such that it refers to another plane*, of which the Greeks cultivate the memory through sacrifice – this 'public thing' that is also called the republic. (This is why the *Prytaneion*, as hearth of the city, is also the place of sacrifice as the edifice where the *Prytaneis* are reunited, that is, the *bouleutes* representing the *demes* that emerged from the reforms of Cleisthenes, and who sit in council in the *Bouleterion* built in proximity to the *Prytaneion*.)

The *skholè* is thus the condition of access to that which, like every object of desire, does not exist, but which, here, constitutes *the object of desire of the city*, of the *republic* – an object that constitutes the city in its turn as that public space where the public thing properly speaking appears, namely, the desire for justice, and of which the interdependent condition is shame [*vergogne*], which is more often translated by *la honte*, modesty or honour, and which is not guilt but *the knowledge of that which signifies the situation of mortals* between beasts and gods, between pure subsistence and pure consistence, as knowledge of this condition. As such, the *skholè* is therefore also what transforms, as fruit of the instituted practice of *hypomnemata*, the object of desire of the psychic individual, become citizen, into an object of desire of *all* psychic individuals. It is, in other words, their 'public thing', that is, their *commonality*, the 'thing' of their common desire, their *koinonia*, which, through this *elevation from the singular to the collective level*, exceeds the particularity of the psychic individual (and which, exceeding the particular, is not simply the universal) and seems to constitute the very process of sublimation as the effective reality of trans-individuation.

For such is the correct interpretation of the law: that which, *making law* in the singularity of interpreting it, makes of this very singularity a new figure of law or right, that is, a figure of singularity *desirable for all*.

The public and collective practice of *hypomnemata* configures politically the co-ordinating conjunction that forms the process of psychic *and* collective individuation. And it does so in such a way that *the other plane*, which was originally the plane of the gods, becomes instead what the philosophers will call, and in all spheres, from mathematics to politics and passing through ontology, *idealities*: this co-ordinating conjunction leads to a new process of *idealization* – and I here take this word, 'idealization', in its Freudian sense.[5]

3. Antigone, the confusion of the generations, authority, and 'the most terrible of children'

Law is usually understood to be what limits or even proscribes singularity, that is, the liberty of psychic individuals, as that which, in other words, *represses* [*réprime*] behaviour that doesn't conform to its letter – and in one way or another all *singular* behaviour tends to be opposed to the letter of the *common* law. Such is the reality of this law, as something that exists and is thus not to be confused with the consistence of justice, the latter precisely being, nevertheless, its spirit, haunting it as that which does not cease returning, a revenance that, however, it *represses* [*refoule*].

That the two planes of existence and consistence are distinct does not mean that what does not exist is cancelled out by the positivity of law, even if things can nevertheless always turn out that way, that is, turn bad, either as tyranny (this was already the destiny of *Oedipus the Tyrant*), as Antigone claims contra Creon, or as that critical and in the end undecidable situation (that is, a situation *that always remains to be re-interpreted*) that is the psycho-social and technical individuation invented by the Athenians, and which as such constitutes (insofar as it always remains to be interpreted) a *tragic* situation. Such distinctions are never definitively acquired, nor definitively severed, and this infinitude is what must always be interpreted anew – always afresh, precisely because this is also what is always threatened insofar as the play of tendencies must constantly compose.

Antigone is the figure of *transgression* and *youth* par excellence, of filial *love* and *fidelity*, and also of fidelity to that tradition that grants a burial to the departed, whoever they may be – which she refers to as a divine law. She thereby represents, but through sublimating them, the tensions between that which belongs to the order of youth – which rebels against the gerontocracy, of which Creon, her uncle, is himself an already old fruit, and in some way rotten – and the memory of 'divine law', that is, the necessity of the archaic as guarantee of the authority of any principle, the oldest and at the same time the most youthful authority, because always re-born, rather than the 'human laws' of Creon – Creon, whose *hubris* consists precisely in not being able to distinguish, within written law, that which is not reducible to it, that is, that which cannot be reduced to the *letter* of the law: justice.

Antigone is sublime because she makes her love for Polynices into the love of the city, even as its undecidable truth, by exceeding that conflict of the generations from which she nevertheless herself derives. This conflict constitutes the ground of her struggle with Creon (and of the opposition of Haemon to his father), the paradox being that the latter, her elder, still holds the position of a youth who has lost sight of the spirit of archaic laws, that is, divine rather than written laws, whereas the youthful girl is the very memory of the most ancient, of principle, who, opposing the 'currentness' ['*actualité*'] of Creon, in some way overtakes him. This is a strange form of confusion between the generations, of which the emblematic figure, in the house of the Labdacides, is Jocasta, the mother of Antigone and of her father Oedipus. Antigone, afflicted with this inherited excess [*démesure*], nevertheless proclaims *aidos* more than any other tragic character: to leave a corpse unburied is to apply the law *shamelessly* (it is to ignore divine law) and to commit in the name of the law the *worst* of injustices.

Antigone is *desperate* [*désespérée*] – she represents an *insoluble* conflict – but filled with a desperate *energy* that she thus, precisely, *sublimates*, calling up divine law, another name for what Heraclitus called *anelpiston*, the unexpected [*inattendu*], the unhoped-for [*inespéré*], the plane of what does not exist but that is nevertheless the object of *any* expectation [*attente*], of all *elpis* – which, in *our* societies, we call hope [*espoir*]. All these are names of desire: there is only law and justice because there is *elpis* (expectation, protention) – because these are nothing other than objects of desire, and because the structure of desire is expectation, but insofar as 'to expect' means to expect the *unexpected*, to hope for the unhoped-for that is inscribed in the structure of what I call an archi-protention.[6]

Antigone's desire is sublimated as the energy of despair. Antigone is herself a figure of *hubris*, opposed to the figure of Creon, and she constitutes *like* Creon a danger for the city. She represents an excess that she has inherited from her father, Oedipus, but an excess which is also the permanent lot of the city – within which we must constantly interpret the difference between justice and law, distinguish without opposing, without cancelling one out in favour of the other, that for which the 'law of the gods' and the 'law of men' are names. But if all this is so, then it is also true that Antigone's despair trans-forms itself into a sacrifice which is itself like the sublimation of that death drive that is called, at times, acting out, the passage to the act, or, more specifically, suicide, from which neither her fiancé, Haemon, nor Eurydice, mother of Haemon and wife of Creon, will escape.

Antigone may not give herself over to death [*ne se donne pas la mort*], but she does commit suicide, take death over life [*elle se fait donner la mort contre sa vie*], and over her desire: she prefers to die, and to renounce the object of her love, Haemon, than to live in infidelity to Polynices and to the laws of the gods. Now, if this *preferring to die* is not simply wanting to die, if it is, on the contrary, the sublime affirmation of a *wanting to live in death* – but *in shame* as the highest expression of life, and very close to death, where life *is* dying, and, as will be the case for Socrates, *in justice*, but then as absolute respect for the law of men which thus becomes piety itself (the piety of Socrates who sacrifices a cock) and which constitutes, again, a paradoxical and sublime transgression (in which consists Socrates' defence during his trial, of which death is the price that he will affirm to the end, and as inestimable, namely, as absolute fidelity to oneself, to one's own law [*loi*], but with absolute respect for the law [*droit*], that is, in respect *to death*[7]) – then this *preferring to die* can appear *in the eyes of those who are without shame* only as a refusal of life, as acting out, as the passage to the act of someone who is desperate, who has lost all reason, and who has sunk into excess.

Here like nowhere else, *aidos*, which is the super-ego par excellence, is very close to Hades, that is, also to the death instinct, where Hades designates not merely the god but also those hells that are his domain (which has very little to do with what Christians will call Hell), where dead souls wander, like demonic powers, revenant spirits, yet weaving the desires of the living – and like the *pre-individual milieu* of the process of psychic and collective individuation, of which this desire is the energy: what Simondon analyses as the milieu 'oversaturated with potential' is what the Greeks think and configure, and as revenance, in their demonic mythology. Here like nowhere else, in this proximity of *aidos* to Hades, which is written in Greek as *Aides*, Eros is entangled with Thanatos. And here, for us, Socrates, who died by his own decision forty-three years after the first staging of *Antigone*, is strangely present – Socrates, that is, his *daimon*.

If, therefore, the authority of the *best* that is justice, insofar as it consists (and this consistence is its *only* authority), clearly proceeds from the critique of law (that is, in some way from its transgression, in the fashion, for example, of that old man, Socrates, the friend of youth), and from its capacity to discern and to judge (within) the law – to discern and judge what is just, a critical capacity that proceeds from *logos*, itself the fruit of the public institution of the practice of *hypomnemata*, that is, of that which constitutes youth as the future of the city liberated from the gerontocracy – then the young Antigone, daughter of Oedipus, nevertheless stands up against Creon, in other words, against the written laws of the rights of man, in the name of a divine law that is that of the archaic, but of which the meaning has been revisited through the grammatization of the inherited conglomerate, and which will raise the question of the *arkhè*, of principle, as the philosophical question par excellence, along with that of the *eidos* (of *eidolon*, phantom), which will become the *idea* (and it is not by chance that Greek magistrates call themselves archons). And in any case, Socrates himself judges and discerns in the written word, ultimately, only in the name of his *daimon*. Everything happens as if consistence stands *beyond* the division of generations, and as their very *unity without identity* (it is without identity because it *does not exist*), as if it was *spirit* insofar as it is the *return* of the most ancient into the current, but a *demonic* return that, mostly, passes through the transgression of youth, youth who are rebellious, lazy, and 'enslaved to everything'.[8]

As we shall see, this revenance (without which there is no authority, other than of a tyranny and authoritarianism without future) which, according to Freud, originally derives from the figure of the dead and sacrificed father (which is already articulated in the myth of Cronos, 'the most terrible of children',[9] who seems so near to Chronos and to the dia-chronic) is what connects the super-ego to sublimation in all its forms.

In the twentieth century, the question of the conflict between the generations takes a new turn, in that full modernity emerging from two industrial revolutions, and as the generalization of a process of the adoption of new ways of life that now dominates the process of individuation, and of which young people are, more than ever, the prime target, and the vector of socialization for the whole of society – this being the origin of what is referred to today with this literally obscene word, *'jeunisme'* ['ageism', or the cult of youth].

The tyrant who seizes the law is thus no longer Creon; it is the market that no longer knows any limits, having forgotten the meaning of shame.

4. From Paris-Bonheur to the blank generation

Antigone is already a form of the confusion of generations: she is wiser and as such 'older' than her elder Creon. But she has also 'lost her bearings': in addition to the fact her father is not just anybody but Oedipus who gouged out his eyes, for whom she is the 'staff for the aged',[10] Antigone must find 'her law in herself', from out of her filial and familial, as well as pious, and as such necessarily archaic, singularity, insofar as authority is the very thing that is lacking – and which condemns her to being buried alive.

In Athenian Greece, and already by the time of Pericles, the divine recedes. 'It draws away, the divine', says Sophocles.[11] The crisis of authority is the crisis of an other plane, which will also have been that of the gods. Monotheism arises after the collapse of Athens, then of the Greek and Roman Empires, and via Plato (revisited by Paul of Tarsus), restoring paternal authority, but a paternal authority that ceases to be the tragic law of Zeus, becoming instead the law of *guilt* henceforth represented by the figures of the Eternal Father and of his sacrificed Son, passing through this *agapè* which 'beareth all things, believeth all things, hopeth all things, endureth all things'.[12] After the industrial revolution, however, monotheism in turn collapses: God is dead.

Authority paradoxically finds itself overturned at the point guilt finds itself exacerbated. Hysteria and neurosis take possession of distressed souls, and above all those of women, and of young women, who are, at the end of the nineteenth century, especially in Vienna, it is true, the privileged recipients of these *novelties* [*nouveautés*] that henceforth shape the course of the world:

> Between each motif, each coloured statement, ran a light, gathered ribbon of cream-coloured foulard as a discreet trimming. There, at either end, could be seen huge piles of the two silks exclusive to the shop: Paris-Bonheur and Cuir-d'Or, two exceptional items that were to revolutionize the drapery business [*le commerce des nouveautés*].
> 'Oh! Look at that faille for five francs sixty', Denise murmured in astonishment, pointing at the Paris-Bonheur.
> Jean was starting to get bored.[13]

Nevertheless, already, youth, lucid and precocious, and modern, *absolutely* modern, despairs:

> Here, there is no hope,
> No orietur.[14]

Youth, who in the twentieth century will sometimes be golden, who will sometimes join the International Brigades, who will form the most spontaneous base of the Resistance (that of Armand Gatti), who will be 'cool' [*zazoue*], whose rise was foreshadowed by Isidore Isou, and which the Beatles, the Beat Generation, the hippies, and finally the protest movement will bring to the fore-front of the political scene, just as it will form the target par excellence of marketing – this youth, at the end of the terrible 1970s, that age during which the president of the French Republic began to play the accordion badly on television, suddenly begins covering walls with ominous graffiti, omens of what is referred to as the blank generation:

> No future.

Today, however, in the current epoch in which *jeunisme* is denounced without knowing what this means, generational conflict has taken a new turn.

5. Despairing orphans of the 'sacrificed' generations: symbolic misery and economic misery

The acceleration of technological innovation puts young people in the difficult position of having to *initiate their parents into the reality principle*, which is constantly being transformed according to the functional conditions of new apparatus. They therefore find themselves having to initiate them into those questions through which society is trying, if possible, inasmuch as it is possible, to invent itself, and this is, perhaps for this very reason – owing to this *reversal* of the order of generations – very difficult, if not impossible.

Now, this reversal occurs at the moment of the *crisis of existence* that I have described as *symbolic misery or poverty*, which is, however, also an aggravated pauperization, an endemic unemployment and precariousness, that is, an *economic misery*: an *interminable crisis of subsistence*; a loss of economic efficiency owing to the fact that libido is being captured and diverted towards 'novelties'; and the revelation of the *economic vanity* of the destruction of existences, becoming a destruction of existences that are *hopeless*, in vain, *for nothing – nihil –* a destruction of existences that can culminate only in the destruction of the economy of subsistence itself (the effects of which are being continually aggravated by the 'economic crisis') and which thus *leads nowhere*. Such is the triumph of nihilism.[15]

In our epoch, which is no longer an epoch, which fails to accomplish the doubly epochal redoubling without which no epoch occurs, and this epoch which, moreover, was believed to have begun with the 'Belle Époque', shortly after the appearance of the Belle Jardinière and the Samaritaine (since closed); in our epoch, ruined by so many of these ills, children, and the young people they so quickly become (frequently referred to as the 'sacrificed' generation), those children and youth who often describe themselves as the blank generation, no longer believe in parental authority. 'Sacrificed generation.' The adjective here is very unfair: on the one hand, because it presumes *a priori* that this generation can do nothing better than its forebears, that it brings with it no surprises, nothing undreamt-of or unhoped-for, that it has no relation to *anelpiston*; and, on the other hand, because a *sacrifice without object* is not a sacrifice. Unless, that is, one poses that the *nihil*, the nothing, is an object, *the object which does not exist*, or *the proof of that which does not exist* but which is the *object of desire*: the unexpected as such, the unhoped-for of what does not in fact exist, since it consists. This object is the *object that is lacking* [*fait défaut*]. And 'blank generation' could be translated as: deprived generation, the generation that is lacking [*génération dépourvue, faisant défaut*].

Now, the political question that this raises, beyond merely the metaphysical or psychiatric question, is how to prevent this non-object or this *becoming-nothing* of the object (which is necessarily and surely also a becoming-nothing of the subject, *including* the subjectivity of young people, but also of their parents and their offspring) from becoming the *very object of despair* [*désespoir*] – and of a *hopeless despair far beyond the breakdown of inheritance* [*la déshérence*, literally 'escheat'] and dereliction described by Christ on the cross as abandonment, that is, banishment [*mise au ban*].[16] (It is usually the loss of *paternal* authority that is mentioned, since this is how authority has, historically, been presented in Western society. But this is clearly not the case for all societies, and one should thus refer to parental authority rather than paternal authority, including in the West, to the extent that primary identification is indifferently attached to the mother and the father[17] – which means that there is a maternal authority, regardless of the transformations that may occur in the succession of secondary identifications that will form the young mind.)

Increasingly deprived of work (other than 'menial jobs' [*'petits boulots'*]), the young men and women of the hyper-industrial epoch find that where there is work, those who are older are unfairly preferred, an effect of the new character of the conflictual confusion between the generations. But these young men and women are also and above all deprived of the possibility of acquiring spontaneous respect for their own parents, which is also to say, for their ascendants, the dead and those who will die, authorities who par excellence formed the Law, from the divine laws that, before the advent of monotheism, with its familial orientation and principle of guilt, were themselves the conditions of the consistence of positive law. Antigone calls these laws 'inviolable' [*'intangibles'*]: 'For these have life not simply today and yesterday, but for ever, and no one knows how long ago they were revealed.'[18] The fact that no-one witnessed the birth of these laws, which are those of desire insofar as it cannot *not* be the desire FOR JUSTICE, and insofar as the law of desire is tragic, nevertheless does not prevent Freud from attempting to reconstitute their genesis.

I will not be able to go deeply into this question in the present volume,[19] but in the third volume I indicate, in commenting upon and criticizing Marcuse's *Eros and Civilization*, why the Freudian questions of the super-ego, identification, sublimation, the pleasure principle, the reality principle, the drives, and generational conflict and confusion can be correctly posed, especially in the epoch of biotechnologies and reproductive technologies, only on the condition of considering the *function* of *tekhnè* in the constitution of this specific form of life called 'existence', and which is configured through generations, cultures, and civilizations, in a *succession of libidinal economies*. For each of these libidinal economies, its *artifices*, as supports of projection, form its effective conditions, insofar as they articulate a succession of de-functionalizations and re-functionalizations – a *general organology* supporting the libidinal economy.[20]

Marcuse understood that there is such a *historical succession* of libidinal economies. But he failed to grasp that this succession is conditioned by the individuation process of the technical system, and that desire occurs only through the technicization of life. Consequently, his interpretation of the question of the drives in *industrial* civilization was incorrect, an interpretation that, with the slogan 'liberation of the instincts', nevertheless greatly inspired the youth of the 1960s, becoming a reference point of May 1968 and also the origin of the discourse of desublimation, a discourse that, through marketing and ideology – including the ideology of the post-industrial society of leisure, and hence also including postmodernism – legitimated the spread of flexibility (of modulation, according to Deleuzian analysis) in control societies.[21]

In this epoch of control societies, parents are stripped of knowledge. Or rather, even when this hasn't occurred, because they happen to belong to that (shrinking) portion of the population that continues to practise a genuine art or skill, something almost unimaginable for their children – with the exception of oligarchies, to which 'elites' are attached, awaiting their crumbs – these parents nevertheless still seem in the eyes of their descendants to be stripped of knowledge, because they are structurally lagging behind the process of technical individuation, and thus the process of psychosocial individuation that adopts the novelties of technical individuation. Now, within the mode of life which is named existence, that is, which accedes to the plane of consistences, a being stripped of knowledge is equally stripped of authority: knowledge *alone* (but knowledge in all its forms – *savoir-vivre, savoir-faire, savoir lettrés*) confers authority.

This 'youth', then, who form *above all and as such* the 'sacrificed generation' (or rather, today, two generations: the 'sacrificed generation' now have children, and *grandparents find they have no authority over either their own children or their grandchildren*), have at the same time become more and more economically dependent on these parents, who have become so difficult for them to respect – and who are so often the source of derision, accused of being 'dowdy', 'squares', or 'clueless', on television, or owing to unemployment (and it has also become normal and quotidian, especially in the wake of Claude Allègre, Lionel Jospin's former minister, to ridicule those to whom the Republic had delegated a part of parental authority, that is, teachers). These young people suffer from a psychological situation in which they have lost confidence in themselves, no longer believe in the authority of their parents, and are confronted with the *structural cynicism of the society* in which they live, a society that produces a world without shame. In this confrontation, they are like symbolic orphans, having to initiate their *parents*, who precisely do not *appear* to them *as* such, that is, as *symbolic figures of authority*. This psychological situation induces a distrust in relation to their own future, and to their everyday existence, an existence that – preceding Claude Lévi-Strauss, who, on his way to becoming the great elder, will himself eventually proclaim, thirty years later, 'no future'[22] – they already no longer love, if they ever loved it: this is a generation *psychiatrically* confronted with a situation of *extreme danger*.

But, faced with such a psychiatric pathology, the response can only be *political*. And this must be a politics of the object of desire, that is (and this will be the subject of Volume 3), *of consistences and of their cults*.

One might object to the raising of this sulphurous word, *cult*, on the grounds that children and young people have not reached this point, that they love and respect their grandparents, that they love life, that they have hopes and beliefs, and I willingly and gladly agree with such objections. And I myself believe, and I hope, I who moreover love the world, who love my children, my grandchildren, and my parents, who are fortunately still with us, I believe and I hope that my own children, and their children, have not reached this point – and that I will be able to protect them from this terrifying danger, and protect myself at the same time.

Nevertheless, what I have described here in such frightening terms is a tendency, and a tendency that, I fear, is largely dominant. And if I believe my children love me, and know that I love them – and I love them knowing that they love the world from and in this love that I have for them, and that I believe they have for me – I also know, and I know it *with complete certainty*, that they *suffer* from what I describe here as a threat, and do so in the way one suffers, for example, from a polluted climate, from the nauseating, heady, noxious (because inescapable) odour that is exhaled by the milieu in which one lives.

Confronted with this tendency, however, one frequently becomes *afraid* to face up to this reality, to admit to the immense dangers that it entails. Hence that *other* tendency: denial. That is, resignation. What I call the *they* or the *one* is also this *being-fearful* that frequently takes the form of that *they* who believe they can escape from the *they* – those who are waiting for the crumbs, the aforementioned 'elites'. And this is what I am trying as vigorously as possible to combat.

Authority is the condition of all consistence: it designates consistence in general; it is the general structure through which consistences are possible. It is also the object of desire in general: it is powerful (it is *true* power, that of the most profound reasons) because it attracts, and, if one can put it like this, it draws its authority from this auto-power; it is loved and admired, as is the young and sublime Antigone:

> *Chorus*: Yes, you go to the place where the dead are hidden,
> but you go with distinction and praise.
> You have not been stricken by wasting sickness;

you have not earned the wages of the sword;
it was your own choice and alone among mankind
you will descend, alive,
to that world of death.[23]

For the countless figures of *kleos* (glory) who form the pantheons, it confers upon them their brilliance.

Antigone, transgressing the law of Creon in which she sees only authoritarianism without credit (as the rest of the city also tends to do, as Haemon says to his father Creon), *makes* authority – and, as a figure of transgression as well as a figure of fidelity to the most ancient, to the archaic as the singularity of the transindividual that she names the divinity of laws older than those of humanity, she *transindividuates*: she links the power of rupture to the *arkhè* of what we must call the super-ego, she *makes* authority by *making herself into an object of interpretation*, 442 years before Jesus Christ – Jesus, who was himself condemned, killed on the cross, and sacrificed 399 years after Socrates (as Paul of Tarsus will read in Plato) drank hemlock.

6.   Witnesses of despair: suicidal society and the politics of terror

A worker in the car industry may have an interest in the existence of cars through receiving an income, even without himself possessing a vehicle. If Henry Ford found a way for his workers to become capable of purchasing a T-model Ford, this was primarily in order to enlarge his market, but as a consequence a new human community was formed, founded on the generalization of automobile use: this technical and human community, which became a genuine *civilization of the car*, is North America, which simultaneously invented the modern consumer and the Californian conurbation, the latter having now been transformed into that social desert governed by a certain muscular Hollywood hero.* The future of this civilization, if it has one (which is probable and which we must hope for), is already to a large extent Korean and Chinese. This

---

* *Translator's note*: A reference to Arnold Schwarzenegger, who was governor of California at the time of writing.

new form of community, in which the automobile reigns supreme, was for a long time the subject of great expectations: those of the *American dream*, a dream that today is evaporating.[24]

It seems increasingly plausible that it will soon no longer be possible to speak of such an epoch – of which the car was in some way the foundation, occurring at the very moment that in France was called the Belle Époque, just prior to the First World War – other than in the past tense. Besides the depletion of hydrocarbon resources, current industrial and technological development, having reached the stage of what I call hyper-power,[25] seems to have passed the highest point of a curve, such that *increases in power have become proportional to decreases in trust* (whereas the opposite was true during the ascending phase of this curve), and this is leading, in its extremity, to despair. If so, this means that increases of power become, in actuality, but via a formidable *après-coup*, increases of impotence. This mechanism (an infernal machine that can be taken as, or made to pass for, conspiratorial machinations) leads to the irrationality of hyper-power.

And this means that the system is on the verge of becoming blocked, or is in the process of changing, and it means in particular that the relations between the global technological system and the other systems – the social, psychic, and geophysical systems – are evolving in such a way that they will eventually be entirely recon-figured in order to adjust to a hyper-powerful technical system. This would be a system, however, that is no longer capable of producing a prior, spontaneous trust, and in relation to which it would therefore be necessary to undertake *exceptional measures*, for example, and in the first place, in terms of policing and the military. It would inevitably lead to a *state system of totalitarian terror*, a *politics of terror* to counter the terror of those in despair, with or without doctrines, isolated or in networks, operated by remote control or emerging spontaneously as a horrifying new generation – white, Christian, and educated, as at Columbine; or foreigners belonging to other faiths and trained as pilots, as in New York in September 2001; or English (but of Pakistani origin) welfare recipients, as in 2005 in London; or French, with or without religion, like Richard Durn (ex-ecologist) or Maxime Brunerie (extreme right-wing militant), all these just in the last few years – *and all suicidal in some individual or collective way*. As for what took place in November 2005 on the outskirts of French cities, I shall return to that in the following chapters.

All this has already been going on now, in France and elsewhere, for several years, as those who are suicidal in these kinds of ways have learned to manipulate hyper-powerful technologies, which have become commonplace and the spread of which cannot be prevented, turning them into hyper-destructive technologies, the future uses of which will be conditioned by human milieus as much as by the geophysical milieu that one calls nature. But as for 'human nature', there is none: it is a *process* of culture, that is, of elevation, of *maintaining* a *desire for the most high* which, if it does not find in a super-ego the authority that binds such desire as the very energy of socialization, and that passes through the possibility of sublimation granted to all individual desires, and if necessary of sacrifice (but a sacrifice must have an object), invents itself *from motives that, departing from the search for the better, lead to the worst.* When desublimation liquidates the super-ego, desire gives itself new figures. But it then becomes the hideous beast [*la bête immonde*] of all abominations, liberating that which takes the form of *negative sublimation.*[26]

The horrific effects of this suicidal tendency – both individual and collective – characteristic of the contemporary, cynical, and shameless world, the horrific effects, in other words, of the death drive, which mechanically induces the exploitation of the drives through a capitalism that ruins the libido, are all the more frightening in that they accumulate at the same time that we are *reaching the limits* of this *global* system (*global* being understood here in the sense of *terrestrial*) that the industrial, technical, and human system forms with the geophysical system of the planet. This geophysical system involves the diversity of local geographical systems, defined by their characteristics in terms of natural resources, climatology, and so on, natural systems that are, in turn, structurally disadjusted in relation to the system of hyper-power (and it is precisely as such that there are passages to the limit).

Now, reaching such limits, combined with the voraciousness of global financial capitalism – which tries to constitute a hyper-powerful oligarchy, producing a reign of terror in order to maintain this hyper-powerful industrial system that is nevertheless becoming obsolete because it is incompatible with rational

existence, that is, an existence that would be desirable in that
it produces motives for living – results in unprecedented geopolitical distortions, that is, literally intolerable *injustices*, in
the eyes of anyone endowed with what is generally called moral
sense, but which I prefer to call shame, the 'shame of being
human'.

This is an intolerable situation – above all, obviously, for those
subjected to these injustices, and *humiliating* both for the people
involved and for the historical and religious cultures to which
they belong – and one that inevitably results in the proliferation
of irrational, demented, and murderous acts, bearing that very
specific death drive that one calls terrorism, and that will only
increase to apocalyptic levels if industrial democracies do not
take radical measures in their *own* lands (I mean: in regard to
themselves), and in strongly demanding them, and before *all* other
initiatives.

These suicidal acts – since Columbine in particular, but foreshadowed by the crime of Corporal Lortie in the National
Assembly of Quebec on 8 May 1984 (after his arrest stating that
'the government of Quebec had the face of my father'), including
the mass suicides committed by members of several cults, and
up to the July 2005 attacks in London committed by English
citizens and, it seems, on their own initiative (that is, without
having been ordered or organized from afar by some other organization, except, in a way, *telepathically*) – together form a series,
and, in various ways, play out a scene. If the perpetrators of
Columbine seem to have conceived their 'scenario' like a
Hollywood movie, displaying at its centre the gaping chasm that
is the very absence of any motive, other acts are accompanied
by various commentaries, in all sorts of forms. But silence can
also send us to other references that are all the more distressing
insofar as they remain uncertain.

I believe, however, that in all these cases, including that of
Columbine (to say nothing of Lortie's delirium), these passages
into action are lived by their authors, in one way or another, as a
form of *testimony*, and even as this need to do evil in order to
have, at least once in their life, the feeling of existing, a feeling
which, according to the testimony of Richard Durn as set down
in his private journal, was then transformed through being acted

out, through the passage into action. For this is indeed what it means 'to ex-sist': 'to testify', here, means to attest before others to a 'disposition', to confront a legacy by leaving a legacy oneself, and through death given as well as through one's own death – which is always in one way or another a testament, even if only through the fear it inspires. If this is true, it means that all these acts tend to evolve towards the figure of the martyr.

3

Spiritual Misery and Reasons for Hope

Man is this animal [...] who raises himself above [...] through his [...] dreams [...]. [M]an is incessantly and necessarily opposed to *that which is* through caring for *that which is not*.

Paul Valéry, 'The European'

1.   The super-ego as necessity of being-by-default (being-intermittently), and the lack of super-ego: from control societies to uncontrollable societies

The normal psychological structure of youth, and in particular of adolescence, is transgressive. But it is also *'hyper-super-egoic'*, especially when it is confronted with parenting (that is, a law) that seems unjust and unfaithful to the spirit of the law, that is, to justice – when it is confronted with what it qualifies as injustice. Youth may at that point discover rebellion (against authority, in its eyes discredited), and it is open to those discourses that know how to channel this rebellion by opening horizons of sublimities – the mirages of mystagogues and demagogues of all kinds, or objects that do not exist but nevertheless consist, and that are thus, as objects of 'care for *that which is not*' (as Valéry put it), the conditions of consistence of existences. And this is what gives to youth its *genius*, through which objects of spirit are produced (of spirit, that is, of the ghost, the revenant, that which returns, makes a return, and always as the repressed, and I shall return to this elsewhere[1]).

Whatever these objects may be, spirit always looks like a mirage, and the converse is unfortunately equally true – not all ghosts are created equal. And this is why some of those whom we think of as suicidal do not themselves see it that way: they tend rather to see themselves as martyrs – thus the way they represent themselves, to themselves and to others, tends to be through the figure of the *witness*. Martyrs bear witness, they testify, above all to their faith, that is, to a kind of collective *hyper-super-egoization*, and, according to the canonical definitions of the martyr, to the ordeal by death or prison. Antigone was such a figure ahead of her time, and this is how she gains her authority, like Socrates and like Jesus, and like all the early Christian saints.

The system of hyper-power is in truth hyper-vulnerable, and trust seems to decrease with every increase of 'power' that is also an increase in the vulnerability and irrationality of the system. This is, then, in reality, merely the growth of impotence, and the excrescence of the absurd, of the aberrant and murderous behaviour that results from this situation, behaviour which is essentially suicidal, but where *the destructive drives tend to be 'rationalized'* by projecting the return of the sublime and of spirits, producing an *energy of desperation* that is all the more dangerous in that it unleashes a combination of mimetic powers, and this is why the 'war against terrorism' will be lost by the populations subjected to this terrorism. As for the powers leading this war, on both sides, both the terrorist networks and the governments of states tempted by a politics of terror, they mutually and temporarily profit from it, and this is the very reason the war is conducted in the first place.

If this growth of impotence continues, and the loss of trust from which it proceeds and which it engenders, thereby forming a vicious circle, and if this disbelief, miscreance, and discredit that result from it also continue, and that inevitably appear as the *generalized and despairing reign of cynicism in all its forms*, then barbarous acts, presented as testimonies to the intolerable, will in the future only proliferate, with the growth of the feeling of injustice and the disappearance of all reasons for hope – reasons that I name motives, and that project the protean consistences that a civilization must cultivate, through which the super-ego is formed, and without which it would be incapable of having any authority.

Miscreance, disbelief, and discredit result from the fact that the super-ego, tending to become purely repressive, no longer has any relation to the authority of consistences, which leads to the destruction of the super-ego, and correlatively to the destruction of libidinal energy. This destruction of motives for existing, which constitutes symbolic misery by dragging existence down to mere subsistence, also engenders – in particular for those who are also subjected to economic misery, and who are thus unable to receive whatever compensations there may be in over-consuming subsistence items, or in addictions, either of which may anaesthetize us to the loss of individuation – either violently desperate expressions of suffering or compensatory forms of delirious and murderous hyper-super-egoization, acting out shamelessly and without the slightest fear, transforming the demotivation and irrationality that reigns in control societies into the energy of desperation, that is, an uncontrollable energy and, in fact, like it or not, a practically inexhaustible energy, that is, an invulnerable energy.

Make no mistake: the French riots of November 2005 were a call for help, just like those suicide attempts carried out by adolescents. Those who prefer not to know, or who refuse to hear these calls, will bear a heavy responsibility – because in so doing they are preparing the way for a far more serious stage of violence. The energies of desperation – found not only among terrorists but also among all those who commit suicide (and who not only attempt it but actually carry it out, accomplish it) and who tend to 'sublimate' themselves (and to thus offset, to compensate for, the process of desublimation) at the cost of all manner of massacres, variously staged – are the liberation of the death drive in its pure state, resulting from the unleashing and unbinding of the drives, itself emerging from the unlimited and destructive exploitation of libidinal energy by hyper-industrial capitalism. This is why they lurk *everywhere*.

When a child looks upon a parent and sees a figure of authority, what he or she sees, through the parent, is the *return* of the succession of generations that no longer exist, but which insist, and this revenance opens perspectives on that which, not existing, nevertheless constitutes the framework of existence as that which, in existence, consists. Such a succession of generations, which may present themselves in the form of a family reunion, but which may also be presented through a library, a cemetery, or a photo album, a house or a monument to the dead, is also what supports this authority that authorizes, this authorization that opens a world, and the words of spoken language are also and to this extent a support. Just like the 'clothes' of custom and habitation [*les habits de l'habitude et de l'habitation*], each word was, once upon a time, tried on (spoken) for the first time, including the names of gods, for example, but these are, however, the names of gods only insofar as they manage to bury this first time; then they are repeated, and insisted upon to the point of becoming common nouns, and it is through these and through their insistence, which is their revenance, that is, also their spirituality, that language consists.

I have elsewhere argued that a word is a secondary retention that has become collective, and that, metastabilized through the psycho-social process of individuation, is 'tertiarized', like everything that supports the authority of the succession of generations, and in which pre-individual funds of individuation consist. And this is why, arising from these pre-individual funds, *authority looks at the child through the eyes of the parent*, like that ghost whose look, however, is not seen, who looks at Hamlet, and who is himself named Hamlet, that is, the father of Hamlet.

2.   Identification, singularization, and sublimation

In *The Ego and the Id* Freud repeatedly states that the super-ego is constituted – and thereby constitutes that parental authority that *transmits* the authority by which parents are themselves 'identified', or, rather, *through which they are individuated* – through *primary* identification, which over-determines all *secondary* identifications: '[T]he effects of the primary identifications made in earliest childhood will be general and lasting. This leads us back to the origin of the ego ideal; for behind it there lies hidden an individual's first and most important identification, his identification with the father in his own personal prehistory.'[2] (This is where Freud adds a note specifying that it is in fact a matter of parental identification, not yet, at this stage, sexually distinguished between father and mother.) As for secondary identifications, they constitute modifications of the ego through the introjection of its objects:

'[T]he character of the ego is a precipitate of abandoned object-cathexes and [...] contains the history of those object-choices.'[3] This identification – which, as introjection, always passes through the abandonment of a libidinal object – is a process that 'narcissizes' the libido: 'When the ego assumes the features of the object, it is forcing itself, so to speak, upon the id as a love-object and is trying to make good the id's loss by saying: "Look, you can love me too – I am so like the object." '[4] Now, this means that *identification cannot be dissociated from sublimation*:

> The transformation of object-libido into narcissistic libido which thus takes place obviously implies an abandonment of sexual aims, a desexualization – a kind of sublimation, therefore. Indeed, the question arises, and deserves careful consideration, whether this is not the universal road to sublimation, whether all sublimation does not take place though the mediation of the ego, which begins by changing sexual object-libido into narcissistic libido and then, perhaps, goes on to give it another aim.[5]

Jean Laplanche and Jean-Bertrand Pontalis have emphasized that this question of sublimation remained in suspense within Freudian theory,[6] and it is my belief that, in fact, this suspense hangs over the difficulties our current age faces in thinking the process of desublimation and, more generally, capitalist libidinal economy.

One of these difficulties lies in the question of knowing whether the passage from *the drive-based object* to *the object of desire* does not itself presuppose a sublimation, that is, also, a 'narcissization', but where this would not simply be an identification: it would be the constitution of the *object of love* as *object of care*, and, as such, a *singularization* rather than an *identification* (before the grieving process, which is the introjection of the lost object). This singularization would occur through the *retro-projection of the singularity of the ego into the singularity of the object of desire* precisely insofar as it is inscribed, singularly, in the *différance* of an incomparability such that, becoming inconsumable, the object of desire is the object no longer simply of a *jouissance*, but of a pleasure originally constituted by deferring its satisfaction[7] – contrary to what is assumed, as we shall see, by Marcuse.

This structure, *which is also that of the process of individuation insofar as it is inherently incomplete*, is what the play of erotic and thanatological tendencies engenders as the metastabilization of a *psychic* individuation that is also a *collective* individuation, precisely because desire is *immediately* set on the path to a process of sublimation, that is, of desexualization (failing which it is a matter not of desire but of a drive seeking the path of immediate satisfaction). And this is why the process of desublimation that characterizes hyper-industrial society implies the destruction of the libidinal economy as such.

Another problem with analysing contemporary desublimation within the framework of Freudian theory lies in the fact it does not allow us to understand the appearance of the technical object in that life that exists beyond subsistence, that is, in that life that desires (which is also to say, that defunctionalizes and refunctionalizes and that to this extent ex-sists[8]). The *love-object* presupposes the constitution of the *technical object*,[9] which is also the condition of fetishism. The technical object also arises, in its genesis, from what must be called an individuation – that of a technical system as the third strand of individuation, at the heart of which there takes place, in transductive relation to psycho-social individuation, the systemic evolution of objects, the technical system thus not being limited to toolboxes and machines: *all* the objects of the world are inscribed within the technical system of objects.[10] And insofar as the technical object is, then, individuated, and the *support of every possible tertiary retention* (and it is through this that fetishism can project itself), it binds psychic individuation to collective individuation. It is, in this sense, the conjunction between the psychic *and* the collective.

Now, the technical object is also the support of the reality principle, that is, of the *différance of pleasure*. This *différance* is an ex-teriorization, and this means that the object of desire, insofar as it proceeds from the *différance* of pleasure, is the object of an ex-pression and is inscribed in what I have elsewhere referred to as the circuit of ex-clamation, which is the manifestation of the circuit of desire in the process of psycho-social individuation that is ex-sistence. But such a circuit is to this extent immediately dedicated to *socializing* this desire, between its origin in the path to desexualization and the sub-limation of the object of this very desire (sublimation is entailed by *différance*), including and especially as the *sexual* object of a sexual *desire*, and not simply as a sexual drive, and this is what is called love. Love consists not in consuming the object in immediate *jouissance*, but *in taking care* of it, *that is, in socializing it and through that transindividuating it*, in, for example, the familial context – and this also consists, moreover, in idealizing it (idealization, being a moment of this form of sublimation, must nevertheless not be confounded with it).

Thus placed in circulation, desire *constitutes social objects* (which is also to say, social *organizations*) as *motives of individuation*, and projects the singularity of its objects to the level of the singularity of a collective and social individuation process through which the narcissism of the *we* is also constituted. It thus seems that the question of the *we* is not, here, a matter of the *identity* of this *we*, nor is it reduced merely to *identification* with an authority (identification would nevertheless be a moment within this): it is the question of the *singularity* of a *we*, which is also and necessarily that of the *I*s of which it is composed, each time singularly, and which occurs through being inscribed in a process of sublimation that is also the principle of *eris*, that is, of the 'emulation' that is individuation.[11]

3. From control societies of identification to uncontrollable societies of desublimation: the infernal mechanism

Freud emphasized two questions that led him to specify the role of primary identification as an arbitrating factor *in the conflicts that result from the succession of secondary identifications*. If the object-identifications of the ego

> obtain the upper hand and become too numerous, unduly powerful and incompatible with one another, a pathological outcome will not be far off. It may come to a disruption of the ego in consequence of the different identifications becoming cut off from one another by resistances. [Hence arises the theme of] the question of conflicts between the various identifications into which the ego comes apart.[12]

And it is here that *primary* identification plays a *unifying* role, if not indeed an arbitrating role, as origin of the ego ideal.

Now, while the *control of conscious time* by *industrial temporal objects* essentially constitutes a *process of the control of secondary identifications*, today it is primary identification itself that has been fundamentally weakened:

- by the fact of the *loss of individuation that afflicts parents, and now also grandparents*, through the symbolic misery that ruins their existences;
- by the *economic misery* that 'tosses them to the side of the road' – but this is a road which doesn't lead anywhere anyway: as economic misery, *it destroys subsistence as well as existence* (it engenders symbolic misery *for nothing*: without *sacrifices*[13]);
- by the fact that *children*, from a very young age, are now the *prime targets* of marketing and the mass media, thereby short-circuiting parents and more generally those figures introjected by primary identification, and this is especially true of television – which in the first place exudes towards them the *nothing* of the *for nothing* that causes symbolic misery, and exudes this as a poison.

In this way, primary identification is weakened. This may occur directly, by taking aim at the consciousness of youth in the very course of its formation and as juvenile 'available brain time'. Or it may occur indirectly, by undermining the authority that results from parental identification and more generally the authority of *ascendance* and of the *ascendants* of these younger generations, and, in the first place, of parents, for whom their own children become, *primarily*, the *authorized prescribers* of consumption – for example, by concocting car commercials in which children are vested with the *authority of object-choice* at the heart of the family circle. Television thus tries to substitute itself for the primary parental identification that it destroys, and to become the support of primary identification itself. But this could only be an identification without authority (an identification of *nothing*), except by constituting itself as *the automatic authority of the drives*, that is, *as regression* (as *regression to power*[14]).

But it is primary and secondary identifications in their totality that are thereby radically weakened: such identifications are possible only to the extent that the object of desire is projected *as a singular object which does not exist* (which thus has *no existence*) and which constitutes *the very motive of authority*. That justice invoked by Antigone would be one name for this motive of authority, as an *absolute singularity* of that which consists in being infinite, that is, incomparable and therefore incommensurable. Now, the possibility of channelling primary identification processes, aimed at the 'power of the rational', through technologies of control and adjustment, and doing so by targeting the psyche of television viewers from the earliest possible age, rests intrinsically on calculation. It therefore fails to allow the projection of any singularity whatsoever. This is why it can reinforce drive-based potential only by unleashing it, by unbinding it, that is: by ruining the libido precisely insofar as it is the power of binding the drives, thereby unleashing an *infernal mechanism*, as Freud also described it immediately after investigating the relation between narcissism and sublimation, and before raising the question of the *conflict between secondary identifications*, and, therefore, introducing the pre-eminence of primary identification: 'We shall later on have to consider whether [...] this transformation [...] may not bring about a defusion of the various instincts that are fused together.'[15] Such a possibility, if I understand Freud correctly, would be that the division of the ego leads, through 'too numerous' a sequence of secondary identifications, to pathological situations, and induces the *weakening of primary identification*, provoking a *pathogenic form of sublimation*. This is what I have previously called *negative sublimation*.[16]

It seems, however, that the process of desublimation, resulting from an 'unlimiting' of the power of technologies controlling secondary identifications, itself induces frenzied and compensatory sublimation processes, which in turn intensifies desublimation. The vicious circle then becomes an infernal, and literally *uncontrollable*, spiral.

For if primary identification is weakened, and if primary identifications condition and over-determine all secondary identifications insofar as they must be unified within the singular ego – precisely as a unification that is a *singularity* rather than an identity (thus as a structurally incomplete individuation process, as *différance*), that is, *unified through its very singularity* – then the liquidation of primary identification, and the liquidation of that parental process of the transmission of authority that is also called the super-ego, ruins the motives of secondary identifications, these motives being their reasons, which are *always* their reasons *to hope*, and notably those reasons needed by youth when they are in conflict (as is necessary) with their parents and with the generation to which their parents belong. There can be no secondary identification *without reason*, that is, *without motive*: without (singular) objects of desire.

Now, these identifications can enter into conflict, and primary identification is over-determining to the extent that it permits the regulation of this conflict. The consequence of ruining primary identification is that secondary identifications become uncontrollable. And they can then become suicidal processes, comprised of all kinds of murderous 'sublimation' processes, an infernal *mimesis* that I call the Antigone complex. Here is the paradox, limit, and point of collapse of control societies.

Primary identification becomes the prime target of marketing while at the same time – and in the context of a global economic crisis *deliberately maintained* through the 'financialization' of the world, through which some are able to profit from this crisis as do 'war profiteers' from war[17] – the reasons to trust in the 'power of the rational' or the technological and industrial system that implements this power do not cease to diminish. Those who have lost all hope of obtaining any benefit from this system, while nevertheless suffering more than anyone the irritations and pollutions of this system, are more and more prone to adopt irrational and destructive behaviour, desperate and hopeless as they are, living with the feeling of having nothing to lose, that is, everything to gain – everything to gain from what seems to us to be the projection of a life after death.

Here we must, therefore, turn again to these desperados, who are not only the 'excluded' youth, relegated to 'problem neighbourhoods', but all the young and not-so-young who have been delivered over to *'control' by the drives*, and who are more or less suicidal *or parasuicidal*.

4. Parasuicide and risk behaviour: the reign of despair in the suicidal organization of society

What is referred to as 'parasuicide' is related to the proliferation of risk behaviour and constitutes a substitutive behaviour in relation to that 'acting out' that is suicide, and it develops in direct relation to the machines of the technical system that deploy hyper-power. And just like the very specific cases of suicidal behaviour already mentioned, and which try to cause the death of *socially 'suicided'* victims, that is, *victims of the suicidal organization of society itself*, parasuicidal behaviour is generally dangerous to others.

Some of this behaviour seems almost innocuous, such as the behaviour of motorists who flirt with death, which is extremely common – one could even say that the vehicle industry has been encouraging it for a long time, and that few motorists escape it totally. And then there are those who deliberately and spectacularly come close to suicide as such, in a way that resembles Russian roulette. Thus, for instance, the 'game', found in certain areas, of driving the wrong way along the freeway. Some would say that this has always existed, and point to the famous scene in Nicholas Ray's 1955 film *Rebel without a Cause*, in which James Dean leaps at the last moment from a car that he sends careering from the top of a cliff. My response to this is to say that if the death drive is in fact constitutive of desire, and if it affects youth in a specific way at certain stages in their development, then what James Dean revealed is precisely the specificity of this distress *in the age of the car*, that is, in that epoch of which the car is the object, the dark side of what, for Americans as for the entire world, was still, then, *the American way of life*. And I would add that the powerful impact of this scene stemmed from the fact that, at the time, the behaviour it depicted seemed extreme and, as such, extraordinary (although it was thereby revealing something ordinary or everyday), and, in this regard, sublime.

Such forms of behaviour have become far more commonplace today, and are no longer sublime in any way: they are *merely wretched* [*simplement misérables*]. And parasuicidal behaviour linked to the car has now become *social parasuicide*, consisting in torching vehicles, but also, with them, every symbol of a social system in ruins, every symbol of disindividuation, that is, of failure, of that failure to which the psychic and collective individuation of contemporary industrial democracies has been led, democracies whose industrial model is now obsolete.

These manifestations of hopelessness and despair, having become ordinary, having become *our* everyday reality, these pathological behaviours – which are nevertheless faithful reflections of the drive-based models that marketing promotes, and which make it seem as though suicidal actions are seeping into everyday life, a manifestation of the slow *decomposition of the motives for living*, in the ruined milieu of what had previously contained possibilities for existing – signify that the reign of despair, that is, the destruction of every reason to hope, has now become immense and terrifying.[18]

If this reign of despair causes suicidal behaviour to increase, then this desperation can *itself* give rise to desperate *reasons*, that is, transform this despair into struggle, by providing itself with objects of struggle. It may, then, want to become sublime, that is, social. The problem is that it can get mixed up with some *very bad intentions* [*très mauvais objets*] – and it is easy to let these bad intentions circulate, reproduce, and proliferate, more or less mimetically: youth *needs to sacrifice itself*, even when it is not exposed to these evils. Youthfulness is an exalted state, tempted by excess because *essentially transgressive*, and this is where its very strength and beauty lie, as well as its future, and with this future, the future of the entire world: there lies its *humanity*. Because what is experienced by young people as *exaltation* becomes, in those with greater experience, *tenacity, conviction, and patience*, through which pleasure and reality are knotted together, and becomes the authority of those who pass into action – 'action' here being understood in terms of those who work and act, and who transform the world through their practices. Such is humanity, a fact that Valéry enjoined us to reflect upon, in the epoch of 'the fall of spirit value'.

But whether or not such a *maturity of adult belief* exists, whether or not it offers reasons for hope to young people, they still need causes, however deceptive they may turn out to be, because the fundamental character of youth is to *not be cynical*, to not accept the cynicism that can reign in this world, whether this be the reign of what, in Antigone's eyes, is the unjust law of Creon, or that cynical reign of despair characteristic of the epoch of hyper-power, a hyper-power that shows itself to be nothing more than *an effective impotence and an infinite injustice* – therefore ceaselessly reinforcing disbelief, miscreance, and discredit, drive-based behaviour and desperate reactivity, both suicidal and parasuicidal, both ordinary and pseudo-sublime.

Given this extremely serious context, it is the responsibility of the *public collectivity* to provide young people (and their elders, within whom they must find some of their resources) with reasons to hope – failing which the different generations, and firstly the youngest, will find such reasons *wherever they can* or *wherever they believe they can*, even if they are being *deceived*. If society does not provide the objects of sublimation without which it would be incapable of elevating itself or transindividuating itself (because transindividuation, being the condition of what is called the *social bond*, is the outcome of sublimation), it will instead incite desperation, with a far greater need for *explosive* compensatory objects, and will take these objects more easily for its own, regardless of their provenance – from extremist ideologies, religious sects, evangelical churches, clandestine mosques, videogames in which the score is calculated by the death drive, or from 'reality television', which measures how degraded and 'available' brains are for the hype and brainwashing of 'power'.

5. The transformation of spirit through the control of the 'perception-consciousness system' and the system of terror

Confronted with the aberrant and ever more frequently monstrous effects of despair, it is tempting to respond with repressive policies that can lead only to a future in which despair increases, and that can end only by transmitting this despair to the greatest number – all the while giving the short-term illusion of being effective, because they conform to the regressive tendencies of public opinion, tendencies that they reinforce by spreading herdish and stupid behaviour. At the horizon of the irrationality of hyper-power, which is in the end hyper-impotent, lies the politics of terror carried out in the name of the struggle against terrorism. But this is only the most aberrant, monstrous, and as such desperate outcome of *everyday, ordinary* despair.

The irrationality of hyper-power leads to global violence. It accelerates and spreads disbelief and discredit by destroying trust, which has itself replaced and destroyed belief. Trust was slowly substituted for belief when, beginning in the eighteenth century, *the use of calculation to control motives* became the principle and 'spirit' of capitalism. But this is then a contradictory spirituality – a *transformation of spirit*, leading to the 'death of God', which Valéry saw clearly, although even today he remains misunderstood. And when Weber examined the 'sermons' of Benjamin Franklin to analyse the capitalist 'work ethic', he demonstrated that this control consists in making belief calculable, thereby transforming it into trust – but at the cost of destroying the object of belief, which is incalculable.

In the first volume of this work, *The Decadence of Industrial Democracies*, I argued that this becoming is inscribed within the evolution of the process of grammatization, as a major component of that war of spirits that arose out of what Sylvain Auroux analysed as the second technological revolution of grammatization, namely, printing. The printed Bible is an objective condition for the appearance of the spirit of the Reformation – which is also to say, for a new conception of *spiritual individuation*. The Counter-Reformation reacted to this, notably by forming the Society of Jesus and the Missions, which, through what Auroux calls printed 'linguistic tools' (these being, firstly, grammar and the dictionary), made it possible to control idioms and, through them, the minds of the entire world, when, in the course of the colonization that began in the sixteenth century, these minds became readers of the Bible.

Now, Weber underscored the fact that the appearance of these new hypomnesic forms, emerging from printing, while enabling the expansion of reading and writing practices, also made possible the control of production and consumption behaviour, beginning with the proto-capitalism of the first entrepreneurs inspired by the 'work ethic'. These proto-capitalists began to use account books, and this eventually led to the calculating instruments utilized by all commercial operators, making possible, along with the new spirit of capitalism (as a new *negotium*), the beginning of what

Weber described as a process of rationalization (resting on Luther's condemnation of monasticism, that is, of *otium*) – which lies at the origin of the 'power of the rational'.

This grammatization is pursued and extended through the development of 'tool-bearing' machines, that is, programmable machines that reproduce the motor behaviour of skilled workers by breaking their movements down into discrete elements, which Marx studied as the condition of the emergence of the proletariat: mechanization increased productivity at the cost of a loss of *savoir-faire* (or skill), which Simondon will later show to be a loss of individuation. This was followed by the appearance of apparatus capable of producing industrial temporal objects, enabling the reproduction and 'discretization' of perceptual time. This, in turn, becomes the basis of control technologies and, in particular, of the control of secondary identifications, as 'available brain time'.

Industrial temporal objects, in other words, enable *control of the 'perception-consciousness system'*, as Freud called it in *Beyond the Pleasure Principle*, and, at the same time, enable libidinal energy to be captured and harnessed.[19] It is in this way that the figure of the consumer arises, the body and motor behaviour of whom, through which he or she subsists and exists, become a body and behaviour *of consumption*. And it is in this way that consumers tend to lose their *savoir-vivre*, after producers have lost their *savoir-faire* (that is, their know-how, their skill). This stage of grammatization, that of industrial temporal objects, constitutes the stage of the loss of individuation that I have called generalized proletarianization, where it is libidinal energy itself that tends to be destroyed – that energy of which the objects, which are *those of belief*, are now systematically submitted to calculation in every sphere. This occurs, furthermore, at the level of primary identification processes, insofar as the control of identification tends to reconfigure these objects. It is in this way that the 'fall of spirit value' occurs, which Valéry described as a *transformation of the spirit through the objects it has engendered*.

It was from out of the Fordist model – itself emerging from the car industry, and introduced at the very moment that Hollywood was being constructed, and which was concretized and deployed as that global social system that is the industrial system of the 'power of the rational' – that this process was unleashed. And such a system rests, as we saw in the first chapter, on a prior, spontaneous trust. Now, it seems today that the exhaustion of belief – which leads, on the side of consumers, to the liquidation of libidinal energy, and also leads, on the side of those without access to consumption (but who are subjected to the problems and pollutions of this system without being able to expect any benefit whatsoever), to the liquidation of every reason for hope, those excluded from consumption thus becoming uncontrollable – is necessarily *also* the exhaustion of trust, which nevertheless remains the *condition* of the functioning the system. It is in this way that the power of the rational, which has become the hyper-power of the development and spread of control technologies, is inverted, turning into an irrationality of impotence, that is, into a reign of despair in which uncontrollable and aberrant behaviours multiply, making evident the *hyper-vulnerability* of the global system,[20] one consequence of which is the onrush of terrorism.

Terrorism and the politics of *repression* that it induces *together* emerge from the social *regression* in which consists the *general degrading of consciousness* ('fall of spirit value'), treated as a monetizable and calculable commodity in the form of 'available brain time', and it is as products of this regression that terrorism and repressive policies together form a system of terror, itself emerging from a *political economy founded on the systematic organization of stupidity* [*bêtise*]. The system of hyper-power – of hyper-vulnerability – thus shows itself to be a *suicidal organization of industrial society*. For this system of terror can only proliferate within the regression/repression cycle into which hyper-industrial society has entered. And, as a direct consequence, this becomes grafted onto the process of the liquidation of all trust and all hope that this regression is revealed to be, as a process of desublimation – a process that it clearly and suddenly aggravates in a catastrophic way (and this adjective, catastrophic, must be heard here, also, in its mathematical sense).

6. Belief and desire

Objects of belief are not existent, and this is why they are not calculable. And even though they are not existent, they are indispensable to existence: they are objects of desire, which only desires insofar as it fantasizes. Existence is only desire, fictions, imaginations, and realizations of these fantasies which become technical or social realities, that is, spiritual realities – and it was in fact as activity of the imagination that Valéry described the life of the spirit, the capacity to elevate oneself 'through one's dreams', the spirit thus being, like the spirit of competition [*émulation*], 'the spur of the best that is the enemy of the good and that commits us to confronting the worst'.[21]

Objects of belief are objects of desire and, therefore, they do not exist, yet they are indispensable for existence, unless the latter sinks into the reign of the drives, which is also the reign of despair and stupidity. By *calculating* these objects of belief, trust ruins them, because one can calculate only with what is existent. It is therefore a matter of elaborating a theory of belief that is also – as a theory of consistences that hold together on a plane other than existence, while nevertheless conditioning it – a theory of authority and of its revenance, as the ghost-like return of what does not exist. It is a matter of elaborating a theory of belief as theory of spirit (of its revenance), and a theory of reason conceived above all as reason to believe and to hope, and which constitutes a particular part of the theory of desire, which is always a *desiring to believe*.

No society is possible without belief, that is, without motivation, or in other words without reason – political, religious, or cognitive, as we shall see in the final volume – whereas *belief is the social and transindividuated translation of desire*, ordinary desire 'narcissized' as the narcissism of the *we*, what is sometimes called, in a vague and ambiguous way, 'values' (from which derives the well-known 'narcissism of minor differences'[22]). Contra such small-minded thinking of 'values', contra the reign of despair and stupidity from which it proceeds, and contra the system of terror to which it leads, it is a matter of elaborating a new political economy by theorizing the libidinal economy in a new way – new to the extent that the object of desire is a singularity (incomparable and incalculable) and where *singularity is what is cultivated through practices themselves presupposing techniques or technologies*. Singularity is what is being forgotten: it is habitually forgotten – and it is, for example, what artistic, poetic, and philosophical practices *reactivate* in ways that are themselves each time singular, and as that which, not existing, nevertheless consists, but *insofar as* existence opens itself up, that is, *works*.

7.　Taking care of 'spirit value'

Singularity is therefore the object of a belief and, for this very reason, it is something of which we must take care, either individually and psychically (for example, by taking care of a love 'object', that is, of a person) or collectively and socially, by making of this singularity an object of desire such that it organizes and configures social structures and their objects, as social objects. Such care is, then, called sublimation, and social organizations are what, essentially, organizes this care. But as psychic individuation is *immediately* collective individuation, all desire, as the care taken of its object, is *already* a form of sublimation.

The object of this book is to open up prospects in order to *prevent the installation of a system of terror*. Its hypothesis is that industry, the current model of which is exhausted, is nevertheless spawning a new form of civilization: industrial civilization. In other words, industrial civilization *is still yet to arrive*. Industry is pregnant with a new form of libidinal economy which, if it is to make its arrival in the world, can be the result only of a fight, and which will consist in new forms of socializing technological innovation, in the North as well as the South, and as technologies of spirit, that is, as care taken of the singularity of its value, each time singularly experienced by the different societies that form this world. (The value of the spirit has here the value of political economy, in the sense that Mallarmé, like Valéry, projects into spiritual instruments such as the book: this is not the value of 'values', that verbose catchall that flows from economic, political, symbolic, and spiritual misery.)

The disbelief that destroys capitalism resembles what Jacques Derrida described as the paradox of auto-immune effects. As pure calculation, it denies the very possibility of a future, given that the future cannot be calculated because it is essentially indeterminate: a calculable future is no longer a future but just the consequence of the present. The future, as that which *breaks* with the present, that is, with what exists, is *already always projected onto another plane*, one *which does not exist* and which, as such, remains incalculable. And it is only to the degree that the realization of the future in a *new* present bears within it that which *remains* to come, therefore that does *not yet* exist, that this present *presents* something; it is only to this degree that in this present the desire for the future presents itself, in which alone a present can consist insofar as it is an existence, that is, a desire to raise itself, as its excess, and as such as its transgression, and beyond all subsistence.

'No future', as stated by the blank generation, and in some way reformulated by Claude Lévi-Strauss, refers to a specific episode of the Western history of libidinal economy, a history that has become global and as such de-Westernized: the capitalist epoch. But this episode will come to an end, and this end *could* lead to a system of terror. This episode, in other words, is a *dénouement*, or what I have also called a *catastrophe*: credit is ruined on the side of consumers who lose trust, and this loss of trust inevitably ends up affecting investors, who then see immense amounts of accumulated capital, capital that they no longer know where to invest, melt away like snow in the sun, this accumulation then returning to its true state, namely, to its *vanity*, the vanity of an irrational accumulation, *for nothing*, automatic and self-destructive. This loss of trust leads in the end to the decadence of industrial societies as the reign of discredit and disbelief, that is, as *despair, in the face of which terrorism essentially presents itself as a reaffirmation of belief* – as the archaic restoration of divine authority, God's anger, a crusade for the kingdom of infinite justice on Earth, and so on – in short, *as the discourse of Bush and bin Laden, one and the same discourse that held us in its grip in the years after September 11.*

For if God is dead and buried, and if capitalist forces, hitherto called 'reactionary' in order to indicate they were strictly tied to bourgeois values, are now completely detached from such values, then a strange *extreme rightward drift of liberalism* causes the appearance, as ultra-liberalism, of *both*:

- an intensification, wherever possible, of the *liquidation of all forms of singularity*, increasing the free circulation of commodities by annihilating every structure likely to offer any resistance to this circulation through whatever *remains of sublimation*; and

- the systematic deployment of *industrial populism*, to compensate for the effects of this liquidation by channelling the regressive behaviour that it engenders into the development of archaic fantasies that seem to contradict ultraliberal 'modernity', and that are generally called 'values'.

We thus witness so many former leaders of the extreme right become, in France and elsewhere, apostles of ultra-liberalism. And, conversely, so many marionettes from across the political spectrum, who all swear by the market, have suddenly 'returned' to 'values', and to those that are most regressive and repressive.

Such a contradiction cannot be maintained for long without provoking a political catastrophe, leading to ultra-authoritarianism and, inevitably, to war and global conflict, the damage from which would be immeasurable – beyond comparison to the worst we have seen in human history. This contradiction is nevertheless *that of spirit with itself*. Spirit, having become the spirit of capitalism, ends up liquidating 'spirit value': there *is no longer* any 'spirit of capitalism', even if, within capitalism, there are still those who seek to animate a new spirit. Capitalism has *lost* its spirit (or its mind).

This fact, however, is not simply tied to financialization, as Patrick Artus and Jean Peyrelevade seem to believe: if it is clear that there is a dictatorship of the short term imposed by 'total capitalism', and that the effects of this are intensifying, in particular by extracting higher rates of return on investment in the very short term, that is, through an extremely rapid socialization of innovation in the form of consumer products that hence become essentially and ever more rapidly 'disposable', nevertheless the real point is that the libidinal economy is being ruined by making desire the subject of destructive calculation.

At the same time that capitalism has deployed its machine to calculate motivations and control production processes and the perception-consciousness system, however, it has also, as a grammatization process, exposed the fact that *spirit is not some vapour floating between the souls* that it would either cloud over or inspire: *spirit is what the technical organization of matter, that is, what the exteriorization of memory, as tertiary retention, induces as a form of life called ex-sistence*, such that only consistences, projected as the motives of its unachievable and as such in-finite future, enable it to individuate itself.

From the moment the system of terror became the imminent threat, it was necessary to draw consequences from the transformations of the spirit, and from the new understanding we must have of it: we must view the spirit in a new spirit. And for that we must bring about a new industrial spirit, and a new spirit of capitalism, by developing a political economy of technologies of spirit, and as the beginning of a new process of psychic and collective individuation – and first of all in Europe. But this presupposes a new thinking of law and ethics – justice and shame must be placed at the heart of political economy as its *principles* (as political principles metastabilized through the process of hyper-industrial psycho-social individuation),[23] that is, as consistences that must be cultivated and made the object of practices, implemented at the heart of new social organizations, and so that they bring the suicidal organization of society to an end.

Such a politics must take as its principle the systematic struggle against what must be recognized as that *spiritual misery* that is characteristic of our age and that has become unsustainable. This spiritual misery engendered by capitalism now immediately threatens it as the reign of stupidity [*bêtise*], at the very moment we have begun to speak of 'cognitive capitalism' and the 'knowledge society'.[24] Ernest-Antoine Seillière recently wrote the following, in the preface to *Les Dirigeants face au changement* (a book that became so famous): 'The new century marked the end of technological income for the West. Today, it is on human capital [...] that our response to the new international situation is built. Education, training: the knowledge economy is not a hollow slogan.'[25] The stakes of this 'knowledge economy' are here defined as a geopolitical question, which is also to say, as geo-economic, and as being so within an international struggle for the protection or reconstitution of 'income'.

But in this context, other, non-Western economic players such as India, China, or Japan are equally inventive with regard to knowledge technologies. And the point is, then, to know – and by distinguishing, within the West, between America and Europe – what a specifically *European* industrial and political economy of these technologies of the spirit would look like. Thus whereas the former president of MEDEF claims that 'business, [...] with its head in the global and its feet in the local, [...] today represents the organization that is best adapted – and most exposed – to the internationalization of public opinion and risk, to the homogenization of consumption, but also to the very real specificities of institutions and international regulations', I, on the contrary, do not believe business to have become the actor par excellence of this change. For Seillière, 'these analyses seem to sound the death knell for grand industrial strategies. [Today it is a matter of] continuous and fluid adaptation to events and competitors.' However, as I tried to show in *Constituer l'Europe 2. Le motif européen*, this adaptation is ultimately fatal for industry and capitalism: this adaptive model is inevitably drawn into an entropic vicious circle, which itself induces demotivation (and, as such, the 'fall in spirit value'). The implementation of industrial policies in relation to technologies of the spirit can only be a long-term action undertaken by a new and entirely rethought international authority – associating public and private actors in a project that overcomes the aporias of the current industrial organization.

As for the necessity of overcoming this current organization, an organization that does not in fact lead to a knowledge economy at all, that is, to the expansion of knowledge in society, but on the contrary to a process of general degradation, resting on what has become a true industrial populism, it turns out that, in the very book just mentioned that was prefaced by Seillière, Patrick Le Lay shamelessly declares, under the eloquent title, 'TF1 – School of Reactivity': 'The brains of television viewers must be available. The purpose of our programmes is to make these available [...]. What we sell to Coca-Cola is available brain time.'[26] An extraordinary contradiction is clearly visible here: it is through this contradiction that 'capitalism is on the way to self-destruction', to cite Patrick Artus yet again.

In *The Decadence of Industrial Democracies* I argued that capitalism is today what must be defended (against itself) and not what must be combated.[27] This does not mean that capitalism is an eternal truth: capitalism is an epoch of psycho-social individuation that is not yet finished, in which tendencies are expressed in an original way, which constitutes the question of composition, but which could nevertheless come to a very nasty, brutal, and premature end – as the *decomposition* of these tendencies. It is therefore a matter of preventing it from ending very badly, and of finding a path such that this epoch of individuation can follow out a course that ends well, that is, that leads to something else – something that, however, cannot even be imagined today.

In this second volume of *Disbelief and Discredit*, I claim that this path is that of a new spirit of capitalism, that is, a new form of spirit engendered by a new form of capitalism, a new form of political economy, one that implements, through a public power rethought in terms of its principles as well as its purposes, an industrial policy conceived on a completely new basis, and induced by the specificities of what must be analysed as the age of technologies of the spirit. This new industrial civilization will need to take greater care of the 'spirit value' than that capitalism which has indeed become 'cognitive', that is, that made knowledge the first principle of its development – as Marx already anticipated – but, *knowledge being sublimated libidinal energy, at the same time destroyed this knowledge, to the extent that capitalism has destroyed libidinal energy in general and sublimation processes in particular.*

Now, taking care of the 'spirit value' means taking care of desire insofar as it is the energy of transindividuation as the passage from the psychic to the collective, as the conjunction of psychic individuation and collective individuation, via the intermediary of technical individuation. In a context in which technology becomes industrial technology, this means, in other words, that to take care of 'spirit value' is to conceive a political and industrial economy of this spirit.

8.   Of spiritual misery

Politics is *social* organization and, as such, an organization *of belief*: no society lasts (a society, as *process* of social individuation, that is, of social trans-formation, is essentially what is organized in order *to endure through metastabilizing itself* – from the tribe to the empire of 'hyper-power') without *believing in its future*, which, however, remains unknown to it, being structurally incalculable and necessarily indeterminate. For there is no *knowledge* of the future, even though it is a certain relation to the future that gives knowledge its flavour [*qui donne aux savoirs leurs saveurs*], whereas the proto-knowledge of the Great Empires of Egypt, Mesopotamia, and China presents itself in the first place as divinatory practices.

Political belief is precisely belief that affirms this *indetermination* as a *principle*, and in a way as the *principle of principles* (of justice, of shame), instead of concealing it in an origin myth that is always also a predestination – giving rise to magical practices in ethnic societies, authorizing a kind of divination in imperial societies, and leading to the astrological practices of decadent political powers. Political belief poses that these principles *are lacking* [*font défaut*], but that in principle, and precisely because they are lacking, *they are necessary* [*ils les faut*] – and they are necessary *as law and as ethics*. This is why *dikè* and *aidos* must always be objects of interpretation, and call for a hermeneutics, within the framework of laws and rules, which are themselves objects of a political education. It is precisely in this sense, according to which citizens *can be educated* in the interpretation of these principles, even though they are lacking, and even *because* they are lacking, that *political society believes in principles*, rather than in myths or dogmas, that is, in revelations.

Politics, therefore, cannot be *cynical*: cynicism is the liquidation of politics and its replacement by terror, whether liberal or dogmatic (oligarchic or theocratic). And in its principle, as its principle of principles, political belief is essentially non-dogmatic in that it is a *critique* of the social translations of its own principles, insofar as these refer to objects of political *desire* and insofar as they *are lacking and deficient* [*font défaut(s)*]. The critique of the social translations of its principles (law as the translation of justice, ethics as the translation of shame) is an *inventive recollection* of the fact that the objects of political principles do not exist, and that their applications are (and always are) *by default* [*par défaut*].

This critique, then, must be *cultivated* as a spirit, and it is an epoch of spirit: *the critical spirit*. The critique of spirit presupposes practices, practices of *hypomnemata*, supports of a political education without which there can be neither citizenship nor any belief in a political future. The principles of justice and shame must therefore be translated politically by the organization of a law and an ethics which are themselves founded on social practices that create psychic and social individuals capable of criticizing them, that is, of individuating them – to enable them to take action [*à les faire passer à l'acte*]. In other words, the *political* soul is *noetic* and defines itself as such – meaning that it defines itself as logical; it is that soul which has passed from *muthos* to *logos*. And *logos*, itself dis-covered through *hypomnesis*, finds, in that *tekhnè* that is the grammatization process, its conditions of possibility.

Hence the constitution of citizenship – that is, of psychic individuation capable of (noetically) implementing political principles and translating them into social individuation through organizations that are also institutions – presupposes, within the *polis*, teachers capable of granting access to letters: *grammatists*. And just as Hermes is the god of writing, that is, of literal *hypomnesis*, which lies at the origin of positive law, the condition of jurisprudential critique as the interpretation of what there is of justice within law, industrial politics today must re-examine *hermeneutical* questions of justice and shame in relation to a new industrial culture, resting on the practice of those contemporary forms of *hypomnemata* that are technologies of temporal objects and digitalization (which modifies the temporality of these objects – I will return to this in the next volume), and which today enables primary and secondary identification processes to be controlled.

This political necessity is also an economic necessity, in the sense that it is here a question of a political economy of the spirit. It is an economic necessity: (1) because the current industrial model has become obsolete and self-destructive; and (2) because the social *practice* of technologies, beyond merely their *usages*,[28] is the bearer of a promising economic model – of which the free software economy is one specific case.

The destruction of existences, which engenders symbolic misery, leads to the self-destruction of the system of power, that is, to economic misery, through which it becomes clear that symbolic misery and economic misery are mutually endured pointlessly: for nothing. Such is the reign of nihilism. All this, when trust is lost, becomes the *reign of despair* properly speaking. And *this reigning despair means that economic misery and symbolic misery lead to spiritual misery* – for which parasuicide is everyday behaviour.

Spiritual misery destroys the possibility of passing to the noetic act: what I refer to here as spirit is what Aristotle's *On the Soul* calls *nous*, and that soul called human is noetic in the sense that it is spiritual, but most of the time it is spiritual (that is, noetic) only in potential, spirit being that to which it accedes only inter-mittently. Because if such access presupposes an apprenticeship, meaning a practice, through which a knowledge is developed, a *mathesis*, and which expresses a desire, that of the prime mover, or what I call 'motive', then this knowledge can never prevent the noetic soul from *passing* into the act of *regressing* to its mere potential, which is therefore its impotence.[29]

Spiritual poverty is that feeling that experiences the epoch of hyper-power as hyper-impotence, and consequently as the 'incon-sistence' of the world, that is, as the demotivation of the acts com-mitted within it. It turns out, however, that the 'power of the rational' that leads to the reign of despair also implies the *system-atic destruction of consistences*: such consistences are singularities of that which does not exist, but which, even though it does not exist, nevertheless returns, intermittently, through *passages to the act of spirit* (which could also be called its *entelechy*), a return that supports the sublimation process maintaining and maintained by social organizations. 'Passing into action', in the sense of the sub-limation in desire of the motive that animates the mind, in turn constitutes the *authority* of the organizations that sublimation supports and that they support. *Spiritual misery, by contrast, is the organization of degradation and of the reign of stupidity, an orga-nization that works by liquidating the institutions that cultivate these singularities and by monopolizing cultural and cognitive technologies in order to control secondary identification, as well as organizing the destruction of primary identification, and of the object that it transmits, namely, the motive (the reason) of all iden-tification*, as a singular expression of singularity, such that it is not comparable and must be socialized through transindividuation.

It is in this way that *the reign of despair is imposed through the hegemony of a culture industry devoted exclusively to the destruction of singularities*, these being considered barriers to the circulation of commodities, that is, to the adoption of consumer behaviour that conforms to the models for using industrial objects established by marketing. Now, the destruction of singularity, as motive of all motives, is also what leads to the *pure and simple loss of every reason for hope – that is, to populism and terror.*

9. Of reason as reason for hope

This spiritual misery, which may be the scourge of the new century but is nevertheless not inevitable, is thus the pivot of all politics to come. Remaining unthought today, if not unthinkable, it presents itself under the sign of a curse, as an evil against which nothing could be done, an *irrational* fatality in the face of which thought and action would be completely helpless (blank). Spiritual misery seems to be the very reign of impotence *because* this misery or poverty is firstly that of thought itself,[30] and if it seems irrational, this is only because thought *itself* is no longer rational. It has become a *case* of this spiritual misery, and such it will remain so long as it does not manage to think this misery *and its reason.*

Insofar as it is also stupidity, this misery, and the reign of this misery, is 'proper' to thought (if one can put it like this): it is not what can *at times* affect thought, but what affects thought *first of all*, precisely insofar as thinking only 'is' intermittently, and insofar as, as shame, that is, as *aidos*, it is suggestive for thinking [*donne à penser*] and, in particular, for philosophical thinking. Now, 'to think', here, also means '*to act*', and not simply to provide endless commentaries and quibbles.[31]

Thinking is that which thinks its own lack of thought. Thinking is lacking, deficient, faulty: it is the desire for an object that it does not possess, but rather that possesses it. This is why Diotima said that, insofar as thinking is *eros*, it is *penia*.[32] *To think is to be possessed by an object that is so lacking that it does not exist: it is on another plane – the plane of consistence. And the entire problem of the current epoch, which is also to say, of current thinking, is to arrive at the thought that this plane of consistence is constituted only immanently* – that it is not a horizon of transcendence. And this is why we must 'believe in this world'.[33]

But this also means that this plane of consistence is not strictly speaking an *a priori*, even though it is a matter of necessity and is therefore not an *a posteriori*. It appears as an *a priori*, but it appears this way only *a posteriori*: this is the question of what I have called – commenting on the *synthetic a priori* of the *Critique of Pure Reason*, and after the objection I raised in the third volume of *Technics and Time* that the schematism of the transcendental imagination was always already techno-logical – the *prosthetic a priori*,[34] that is, an *a priori* that arrives only *après-coup*, after the fact, that is, *a posteriori*. And this is what it has not occurred to thinking to think, and what maintains it as a particular case of spiritual misery, that is, of that which,

- as the perception-consciousness system,
- as inscribed within identification processes, and
- as activity of sublimation par excellence (and exposed par excellence to de-sublimation),

submits thinking, insofar as it is also and primordially stupid (stupidity itself always being in some way prosthetic), to the hegemony of the culture industries that operate precisely as this *a priori prostheticity*.

There is a *reason* for spiritual misery, and this only appears irrational and only remains (as regression to power) insofar as this misery has not discovered its motive (its reason). My hypothesis is that the motive of this misery is tied to the third strand of individuation (the individuation process of the technical system), and has not been the subject of either thought or critique – nor has it been the subject, therefore, of political action. It constitutes the blind spot of psycho-social individuation, and there is every reason to speak of poverty because this blindness is also the point of collapse of the capitalist political economy. But a thought of spiritual misery or poverty is also and necessarily, and above all, the thought of its own lack: the thought of a necessary, if not a 'transcendental', stupidity.

Thinking spiritual misery must begin by re-thinking how this is a question of spirit, and of its value, that is, its relation to desire, and its realization as social activity within a libidinal economy that is otherwise ruined, and that as such engenders symbolic misery and economic misery. Symbolic misery, as a process of desublimation and generalized degradation, totally destroys the life of the spirit, lowers the value of the spirit to the point of annihilating it, causes the regression of a spirit in conflict with itself, and becomes spiritual misery. And just as it can be said that shame – and its destruction – is not a moral question, nor even purely and simply an ethical question, but rather the question of the capitalist economy as a self-destructive epoch of libidinal economy, so too the question of spirit is not the question of a value outside all values, that is, outside the economy: insofar as it is constituted by *hypomnemata*, that is, by tertiary retentions, the question of spirit becomes an industrial question, and a question of political economy, given that such *hypomnemata* have now become the basic operating system of the hyper-industrial apparatus.

There is only reason as that which projects a motive, and this motive can only be a reason for hope: the motive, insofar as it moves [*émeut*], sets in motion towards that which opens to reason the possibility of its unprecedented future. In other words, reason is a process of individuation – a process that can project itself onto another plane, one that is drawn to that which does not yet exist, or, in other words, to the plane of imagination that forms these *affects* that I call motives, of which reason projects *the unity, as the motive of all motives*.

And yet, as we shall now show, the hyper-industrial epoch *disaffects* individuals: this disaffection, which is inevitably also a de-motivation and therefore a 'de-reasoning', given that reason is a motive and as such an affect, is the highly disturbing outcome of a massive process of disindividuation – that is, of the loss of both psychic and collective individuation, through which it is the very collective itself that is annihilated.

4

The Disaffected Individual in the Process of Psychic and Collective Disindividuation

One is not serious when one is seventeen.
Arthur Rimbaud, 'Romance'

Someone who wants to drown his dog says it has rabies.
Proverb

1. The hypermarket

The political economy of 'spirit value' is that of the libidinal economy – where value, in general, has worth only for somebody who *can desire*: only insofar as it is inscribed in the circuit of desire, which desires only what remains *irreducible* to the commensurability of all values.* In other words, value is worth something only inasmuch as it evaluates what has no price. It cannot, therefore, be *completely* calculated: there is always a remainder, which induces the movement of a *différance*, and only through this can values be put in *circulation*, that is, into exchange. Value has worth only to the extent that it is inscribed in the circuit of individuations and transindividuations, and these can only individuate singularities.

Now, in the hyper-industrial political economy, value must be completely calculable,[1] *that is, condemned to become valueless*:

---

* Translator's note: I would like to thank Patrick Crogan for his assistance with an earlier version of the translation of this chapter.

such is nihilism. The problem, then, is that it is the consumer who is not only devalued (for consumers are evaluated by, for example, calculating their 'life-time value') but also devalorized – or, more precisely, disindividuated. In such a society – which liquidates desire, desire being, however, the energy of society insofar as it is libidinal energy – value is what annihilates itself and, with it, those who, evaluating it, are themselves evaluated. This is why it is society as such that eventually seems to its members, themselves devalorized (and melancholic), as being without value – and this is also why society then fantasizes that much louder and more ostentatiously about 'values' which are merely deceptions, compensatory discourses, and consolations. Such is the fate of a society that no longer loves itself.

The scene of this devalorizing devaluation is not simply the market; it is the hypermarket typical of the hyper-industrial epoch, where commodities, handled 'just in time' through the use of barcodes and buyers equipped with credit and debit cards, all become commensurable. This was the case, for example, at the Commercial Activity Zone (ZAC) of the Saint Maximin hypermarket, not far from Creil, built by the Eiffage corporation (which recently purchased one of the roadworks companies privatized by the French government), a ZAC within which Patricia and Emmanuel Cartier would spend Saturday afternoons with their children. They did so right up until the day, in August 2002, when they eventually decided to kill these children, in order to lead them, according to their father, towards a 'better life' – a life after death, a life after *this* life that no longer produced anything but despair, such desperation that these parents were driven to inject their children with fatal doses of insulin: "'We all had to die." They intended to end their lives, in order "to depart for a better world". "It was a long-held hope."'[2] They consumed a great deal. The prosecutor and children's rights advocate, Caroline Pelouse Laburthe, 'reproached Patricia and Emmanuel Cartier for smoking too much, for giving their children too much Coca-Cola, [...] for letting them spend too much time playing video games'.[3] And then, debt-ridden – they had about fifteen credit cards between them – they decided, a little like the parents of Petit Poucet abandoning their children in the forest, to inject their own children with insulin, then commit suicide themselves, hoping to meet again in a 'better world'. The injection proved fatal only for Alicia, who was eleven years old, and who succumbed after three weeks in a coma.

Does this mean these parents did not love their children? Nothing is less certain. The only thing of which we can be certain is that everything had been done to make them no longer capable of loving them, given that '*to love*' is not synonymous with '*to buy*' – even though the hypermarkets would like their customers to believe that if I love, I buy, and that I love only *to the extent* that I buy, and that everything can be bought and sold. '*To love*', however, is not only a feeling – it is a *relation*, a way of being and living with the one who is loved, and for them. Love is the most exquisite form of *savoir-vivre*.

Now, it is just such an exquisite relation that the commodification of life destroyed in the Cartier family. As I tried to show in the preceding chapter, children are being progressively and tendentially deprived of the possibility of identifying with their parents, because their primary identifications are being diverted and distracted towards industrial temporal objects, as are their secondary identifications, and just as are the secondary identifications of their parents, with the precise goal of causing them to adopt behaviour that is exclusively submitted to consumption (each member of the Cartier family had his or her own television). In the same way, and reciprocally, parents – incited in this way to consume more and more by the combined power of television, radio, newspapers, advertising campaigns, junk mail, editorials, and political discourse that speaks constantly of 'stimulating consumption', not to mention the banks – find themselves expelled from any position from which they would be able to love their children truly, practically, and socially. What results is the diseased love [*mal-aimer*] of a terrifying ill-being [*mal-être*], which becomes, step by step, a *general disenchantment* [*désamour*] – from which even Claude Lévi-Strauss himself was unable to escape.

Our epoch does not love itself. And a world that does not love itself is a world that does not believe in the world: we can believe only in what we love. This is what makes the atmosphere of this world so heavy, stifling, and anguished. The world of the hypermarket, which is the effective reality of the hyper-industrial epoch, is, as an assemblage of cash registers and barcode readers, a world in which loving must become synonymous with buying, which is in fact a world without love. The Cartiers thought their children would be happier if they bought them games consoles and televisions, but the more they bought these things, the less happy they found their children to be, and the more they were driven to purchase even more, and the more they lost sight of the very meaning of filial and familial love: in short, the more they were *disaffected* by the poison of hyper-consumption. Ever since 1989, the year they married and began their family, they were inculcated – to their great misfortune – into the belief that a good family, a *normal* family, is a consuming family, and that such is the direction in which happiness lies.

The Cartiers may have been condemned to ten to fifteen years of incarceration, but they were themselves victims as much as perpetrators. They were victims of the everyday desperation of the intoxicated consumer, victims who suddenly, here, acted out, passed over to the terrifying act of infanticide, because they were trapped by an economic misery that also engendered a symbolic misery. There is no doubt, in my view, that even if it was necessary to convict them, nevertheless such a judgment must precisely analyse and detail the attenuating circumstances, and this judgment can be just only inasmuch as it also and perhaps above all convicts the form of social organization that led to such degradation. Because this organization is that of a society that has itself become infanticidal, a society in which childhood is in some way killed in the womb.[*]

2. Intoxication, disintoxication

Consumption is intoxication: today this has become obvious. And it is highlighted in an article written by Édouard Launet during the trial of Patricia and Emmanuel Cartier: '[The couple lived close to] Saint Maximin [...] the largest commercial zone in Europe [...] at once El Dorado and wasteland, abundance and social poverty. The market, nothing but the market, and

---

[*] *Translator's note*: The usual translation of '*tuée dans l'oeuf*' is 'nipped in the bud', but this does not seem to convey the gravity of Stiegler's judgement.

those little adrenaline rushes that come with the purchase of a television or a sofa.'[4]

Within days of the tragedy of Clichy-sous-Bois that sparked riots across France lasting three weeks, in the Cora hypermarket – site of a 'great social melting pot' where the 'little people' of Beauvais (among them the Cartiers) mix with more 'comfortably off' Parisians, who spend their weekends in their second homes around Gouvieux and Chantilly – in this hypermarket where 40,000 people pass through the forty-eight cash registers and their barcode readers every day, 'Jean-Pierre Coppin, head of store security, observed: "We know we're sitting on a pressure cooker." '[5]

How right he is. This 'mere' security guard knows that the 'immediate consumption' of life brings disorders. And so indeed does Nicolas Sarkozy, who expresses his agreement – in a way, however, that is not without serious problems in terms of the conclusions he draws – in his discourse on hope, despair, and spirituality, that is, on the benefits of religion (I shall return to this in the final chapter): 'In the suburbs [...] within which every despair is concentrated, it is better that youth have spiritual hope rather than having their heads filled, as their only "religion", with violence, drugs, or money. [...] Life is not goods for immediate consumption.'[6] For the immediate consumption of life today provokes suffering and despair, to the point where a profound malaise now reigns in consumer society. As mentioned previously,[7] a survey commissioned by the IRI Institute drew attention to the figure of the 'alternative consumer', among a proliferation of other symptoms of this crisis of hyper-industrial civilization – including anti-advertising and anti-consumption movements, declining sales of brand-name products, and so on.[8] I have often heard the objection that in fact no decline in consumption has been verified (even though the IRI study was undertaken in the wake of a fall in sales of consumer products), and thus that there is no crisis: alternative consumers, that is, those who express discontent with consumption, and who desire to live differently, are in fact often among the largest consumers – tantamount to hyper-consumers. The malaise would therefore be nothing more than the false reporting of bad news.

But there is nothing contradictory about a hyper-consumer denouncing consumption, no more than there is any contradiction in the responses to another survey, conducted by Télérama on French viewing habits and viewers' opinions of the programmes on television. This survey showed that even if 53 per cent of respondents considered television programmes to be detestable, nonetheless most of them watched the very programmes they considered so terrible. There is no contradiction here, because both these cases involve addictive systems, and, as we know, a system is addictive to the precise extent that the person caught within the system denounces it, and suffers all the more from being unable to escape it – such is the well-known phenomenon of dependence.

The 'adrenaline rush' that accompanies a major purchase is produced by the addictive system of consumption, and the same goes for those viewers surveyed by Télérama who condemn the programmes they nevertheless watch, like heroin addicts who, having reached the stage where consuming this molecule brings nothing but suffering, because it has blocked the natural production of dopamine, serotonin, enkephalins, and endorphins in their brain, find temporary relief in even greater consumption of the very thing that causes this suffering – amounting to an immediate consumption of life that can only aggravate the problem still further, until it is transformed into despair, as Nicolas Sarkozy stated. This is why, just like viewers of television who no longer enjoy television programmes, if one asks heroin addicts what they think of the toxic substance on which they are dependent, they will tell you it is the worst evil, but ask them what they need right now and they will reply, over and over again: heroin. Over and over again: so long, at least, as they lack the means to disintoxicate themselves.

Televisual stupefaction, which in the beginning was the hashish of the poor, replacing the opium of the people, becomes a hard drug when, having destroyed desire, it begins to target the drives – because the desire that bound them and kept them in equilibrium has disappeared. This is the change from cheerful consumption, which believes in progress, to miserable consumption, by which consumers feel they are regressing and suffering. At this stage, consumption releases more and more compulsive automatisms, and consumers become dependent on the 'rush' that consuming brings. They then begin to suffer from a disindividuating syndrome for which the only compensation is to intensify their consumer behaviour, which at that point becomes pathological.

This is so because in hyper-industrial society, where everything becomes a service – that is, commodity relations and objects of marketing – life has been *totally* reduced to consumption, and the effects of psychic disindividuation *totally* rebound upon collective individuation, given that within psychic and collective individuation processes, psychic individuation concretizes itself only as collective individuation and transindividuation, and conversely. When everything becomes a service, transindividuation is totally short-circuited by marketing and advertising [*la publicité*]. Public life is then destroyed: *psychic and collective individuation turns into collective disindividuation*. There is no longer any '*we*'; there is only the *they*. And the collective, whether it be familial, political, professional, confessional, national, rational, or universal, no longer bears any horizon: it seems totally devoid of content, which is what philosophers refer to as *kenosis*, and which in turn means that the universal no longer refers to anything other than the market and the technologies that have expanded across the entire planet – to the point that the Republic, for example, or what pretends to replace it, or bolster it, or reinvent it (for example Europe), is no longer loved or desired.

3. Disaffection and withdrawal

Hyper-industrial society is intoxicated, and the most pressing political issue is the question of disintoxication. Intoxication is the result of 'saturation', which particularly affects the higher functions of the nervous system: conception (understanding), perception, and imagination, that is, intellectual, aesthetic, and affective life – *the mind in all its dimensions*. Here is the source of every form of spiritual misery. Call these the cognitive and affective forms of saturation typical of hyper-industrial society.

Just as there is *cognitive saturation* (there have now been over ten years of research into the effects of 'cognitive overflow syndrome', with the paradoxical result – paradoxical, that is, for a narrowly 'informational' conception of cognition – that the greater the information delivered to a cognitive subject, the less he or she knows[9]), so too there is, indeed, *affective saturation*. Cognitive and affective saturation cause individual and collective, neurological and psychological, cognitive and personality, *congestion*, comparable to the paradoxical effects of the urban congestion that results from excessive traffic, the most common of these effects being traffic jams, where the car, intended to facilitate mobility, on the contrary produces noisy and polluting – that is, toxic – slowdowns and paralysis. Just as cognitive saturation induces a loss of cognition, that is, a loss of knowledge, and a confusion of minds, stupefying consciousness so that it becomes increasingly unconscious, so too affective saturation engenders *generalized disaffection.*

Cognitive and affective saturation are therefore cases of a larger congestive problem, afflicting all hyper-industrial societies, from Los Angeles to Tokyo to Shanghai. When Claude Lévi-Strauss said he was preparing to say goodbye to a world he no longer loved, citing demographic explosion, he presented a case of this generalized intoxication: 'The human species lives under a sort of regime of internal poisoning.'[10]

In all these cases of congestion, humanity seems confronted by a phenomenon of disassimilation, comparable to what Freud described among protists, referring to the work of Woodruff:

> [I]nfusoria die a natural death as a result of their own vital processes. [...] An infusorian, therefore, if it is left to itself, dies a natural death owing to its incomplete voidance of the products of its own metabolism. (It may be that the same incapacity is the ultimate cause of the death of all higher animals as well.)[11]

Moreover, and I shall return to this in the final chapter, that sclerosis that can become the super-ego, like morality, can also engender such self-intoxication.[12] The intoxication produced by affective saturation (this was undoubtedly one element lying at the origin of the crime of Patricia and Emmanuel Cartier), however, constitutes a case of congestion far more serious and worrying than any other: a congestion that affects the reflective and decision-making abilities of psychic and collective individuals, but also their capacity to love their relatives and friends, to love them effectively, practically, and socially, a congestion that inevitably leads, in the end, to very serious problems of political hatred and violent conflict between social groups, ethnicities, nations, and religions, and that makes virtually inconceivable any potential solutions to the other kinds of congestion that poison every aspect of life on the entire planet.

Affective saturation results from the hyper-solicitation of attention, and in particular the attention of children, and aims, through the intermediary of industrial temporal objects, to divert their libido from their spontaneous love objects exclusively towards objects of consumption, thus provoking indifference towards their parents and to everything around them, as well as a general apathy, overlaid with a sense of threat – of which the monstrous heroes of Gus Van Sant's *Elephant* are symbols, or rather 'dia-boles'.

In Japan, where I find myself at this moment writing this chapter, the congested reality of psychic and collective disindividuation leads to acting out [*passages à l'acte*], televisual and criminal mimetisms, and an absence of shame, *that is, of affection* (for instance, the two young Japanese criminals who, asked to express repentance for killing their victims, respectively a sixty-four-year-old woman and some young pupils at a kindergarten, both replied that they had no regrets).[13] Meanwhile, the appearance of *hikiko-mori* and *otaku*[14] *constitute two typical cases of disaffected youth, examples of disturbing proportions,* given[15] that there are more than a million *hikikomori*, hundreds of thousands of whom have left school, and are profoundly cut off from the world, living a kind of social autism, ensconced in their domestic and televisual milieu, and hermetically sealed away from a social environment that is itself largely ruined:

> His family life shattered, Mr Okuyama, 56 years old, recalled: 'We were forced to move last May, because it was becoming too danger-ous to stay with my son, due to his violence.' Despite the efforts of the parents, communication is virtually absent. 'I try to meet with him once a week and have a normal discussion, but it is very difficult. He talks only in insults and unintelligible words,' his father explained. 'Also, I'm scared: he's twice as strong as me.'[16]

Almost completely cut off from the education system, they may act out, thereby supplying a substantial and disturbing string of stories to Japanese newspapers: 'In 2000 a 17-year-old boy who had been living as a recluse for six months, having been the victim of bullying and harassment at school, hijacked a bus with a kitchen knife and murdered a passenger.'[17] *Otaku* live only within a closed, virtual world of computer games and comics, and only within that world can they meet their kind: *other otaku*, equally disaffected, that is, disindividuated *psychically as well as socially*, or in other words perfectly indifferent to the world:

> In his latest novel, *Kyosei Chu*, a title that may be translated as *The Daily Life of the Worm*, Ryu Murakami analyses how adolescents, refusing to confront reality, construct a purely fictitious world inspired by comics and animation. They enter this world thanks to ever more sophisticated gadgets, with which Japanese industry saturates them. Unable to communicate with others, these youth spend most of their time in front of a games console or a computer, seldom leaving the house.[18]

Some *otaku* practise a worship of objects, in particular, objects of consumption:

> They organize their existence around a passion that they push to extremes. This can be for [consumer] items: hence the *otaku* who keeps in his room old computers purchased online, or the teenager who possesses hundreds of Chanel bags. Some of these weird cults pose a problem, such as the one that has recently developed around Joyu, spokesperson for the Aum sect that carried out the sarin gas attack that killed twelve people in the Tokyo subway in May 1994.[19]

We urban dwellers (and we are now all, or nearly all, urban), we suffer from this psychic and collective congestion, and from the affective saturation that 'disaffects' us, slowly but ineluctably, from ourselves and others, disindividuating us psychically as well as collectively, distancing us from our children, our friends, our relatives, from *our own*, all of whom are constantly moving away from us. It disaffects us from everything dear to us, everything granted to us by *charis*, by the grace of charisma, from the Greek *kharis*, and from a charisma of the world from which proceeds all *caritas*, which is given to us and without doubt from the beginning (primordially, from the outset) as ideas, ideals, and sublimities. We, we others, we who feel ourselves being distanced from our own, feel ourselves irresistibly condemned to 'live and think like pigs'.[20]

Those of us still fortunate enough to live in towns or urban centres, rather than in the outer suburbs, try to survive spiritually by assiduously visiting museums, galleries, theatres, concert halls, art-house cinemas, and so on. But we then find ourselves suffering from a different illness, cultural consumption, and discover that we must absorb ever more cultural commodities, as if another form of addiction had gripped us, one that prevents us from ever being able to re-establish the slow pace of genuine artistic experience. And so the age of the '*amateur*', the art-lover, comes to be replaced by the consumer suffering from a dazed cultural obesity.

When we do have the chance of getting away to the countryside, a chance to finally 'take a breath', therefore, we suspend these endless, constant, and systematic affective solicitations that characterize contemporary life, where everything has become a service, now almost completely submitted to marketing, including 'cultural' marketing. We thus return to the primary affective solicitations of greenery, flowers, animals, the elements, solitude, the village market, and of silence and a slower pace. This slowness and silence have today been lost: the absolutely incessant way in which the senses are assaulted, with the goal, precisely, of never letting up, induces a saturation that drags us into an age of disaffection [*désaffection*] – and of withdrawal [*désaffectation*].

This loss of consciousness and affect, induced by cognitive and affective saturation, which constitutes the appalling reality of spiritual misery, at the very moment when the planet must confront and resolve so many difficulties, is what characterizes the *lost spirit of capitalism*. Today there are disaffected people just as there are disused factories [*usines désaffectées*]: there are *human wastelands* just as there are industrial wastelands.[21] Such is the daunting question of the industrial ecology of the spirit. And such is the enormous challenge that befalls us.

4. Disturbances

Beyond *disaffection*, which is the loss of *psychic* individuation, *disaffectation* or *withdrawal* is the loss of *social* individuation, which in the hyper-industrial epoch threatens disturbed or disruptive children [*les enfants turbulents*], who are tending to become disaffected individuals. Since the completion of a study by INSERM [the National Institute for Health and Medical Research], however, based on the American classification of pathologies and on cognitive methods linking psychiatry, psychology, epidemiology, and the cognitive, genetic, neurobiological, and ethological sciences, disturbed children are now subject to the nosological category 'conduct disorders'.[22]

These 'conduct disorders' are systematically associated with attention disorders. For attention is also, as Jeremy Rifkin underscored, the most sought-after commodity – for example, by TF1 and its managing director, Patrick Le Lay, who explained that the attention that consists in 'available brain time', and which constitutes the quantifiable television audience, is perfectly controllable and controlled, thanks to the techniques of the ratings system: '[It is] the only product in the world where we "know" our clients down to the second, after a delay of 24 hours. Each morning, we see the fully detailed results of the previous day's operation.'[23]

The disaffection produced by affective saturation, which is thus also a withdrawal, that is, a *loss of place and social recognition*, resulting from the loss of individuation that strikes disaffected individuals, and which is translated into the process of collective disindividuation, is directly connected to the fact that capturing attention destroys attention – and, with it, that quality of *being attentive* (which is social and not merely psychological) that is called, very precisely, shame [*la vergogne*], a sense preserved very well in the Spanish word *vergüenza*.[24]

For *attention is what arranges and is arranged by retentions and protentions*, but today retention and protention are both massively and continuously controlled by the retentional and protentional processes of television. From the childhood stage of primary identification to the secondary identifications of the adult, these processes seek to replace the secondary collective retentions elaborated through the process of transindividuation (in which consists the life of a psychic and collective individuation process) with collective secondary retentions entirely fabricated according to the results of market research and marketing techniques, as well as the specifications of designers, stylists, developers, and ergonomists, together producing the accelerated socialization of technological innovation.

The INSERM study that defined this pathology of 'conduct disorders' (based on North American categorizations) is open to question to the extent that it seriously neglects the fact that attention has become a commodity. Yet despite this neglect, this study classifies a 'conduct disorder' (referring to behaviour that transgresses social rules) as a mental disorder only if it is accompanied by other symptoms, in particular attention deficit disorder or 'oppositional defiant disorder': 'Among the psychiatric pathologies most frequently associated with conduct disorders are attention deficit/hyperactivity disorder [and] oppositional defiant disorder.'[25] Children or adolescent sufferers also frequently suffer from depression and anxiety, and they can readily progress to suicide.

The study claims to have identified an empirical probability that such disorders will develop connected to the following factors: 'A family history of conduct disorders, criminality within the family, very young mothers, substance abuse, etc.' Based on this, 'the panel recommends the identification, during the course of the medical monitoring of pregnancy, of families possessing these risk factors'. It further recommends 'developing an epidemiological study of a representative sample of children and adolescents in France [and] conducting targeted studies of populations at high risk (a history of imprisonment, children in special education, disadvantaged urban areas)'.[26]

The real issue is the destructive effects on both psychic and collective individuation that result from affective saturation and the various forms of congestion that poison and intoxicate contemporary society, especially television, *which is devastating the attentional faculties of children, adolescents, their parents*, and adults in general, notably including politicians – and perhaps the INSERM researchers themselves, who no doubt themselves watch TV.

The study, which shares cognitivist assumptions that grant an essential role to genetics, and therefore to hereditary factors, is not unaware of the fact that it is necessary 'to evaluate the specific role of both genetic and environmental susceptibility in conduct disorders'. And, while recommending research into 'genetic vulnerability', it also recommends 'studying the influence of parental attitudes'.[27]

While they are not going so far as to suggest that parents who present with these risk factors ought to be sterilized, we cannot help but recall that several American states (America being the country whose classification of mental diseases clearly formed the basis for this study) carried out such sterilizations before the war, and ceased doing so only after the revelation of the Nazi horrors.[28]

Why not propose to study the influence of television, and of the innumerable techniques of incitement to consumption that are the cause of affective saturation syndrome? Television does indeed receive a mention: 'Recent studies confirm that being exposed to violence on television from the age of eight is highly predictive of aggressive behaviour in the long term [...] and this relationship holds after controlling for the IQ or socio-economic status of the subjects.'[29] But this fails to grasp the influence of television for what it is: the effect of an industrial temporal object that enables attention to be captured and harnessed, which that enemy of beauty* refers to as 'available brain time'. What credence should be given, then, to a psychopathological study that claims to describe the problem of the loss of attention, but that itself pays no attention to the techniques through which attention is captured?

The question of the psycho-social environment is that of the process of psychic and collective individuation, over-determined by the process of technical individuation, especially in an epoch in which technics has largely become an industrial system of cognitive and cultural technologies, that is, of what I and my colleagues at Ars Industrialis[30] call 'technologies of spirit'. It follows that the dysfunction of psychic, collective, and social individuation processes must be treated more as questions of *sociopathology* than of *psychopathology*.

Translator's note: The author is referring here again to Patrick Le Lay (the director of TF1, who infamously referred to his job as selling 'available brain time' to Coca-Cola), and playing on the phonetic similarity between his surname and *'le laid'*, 'ugly'.

5. From psychopathology to sociopathology

It is clear that the psychopathological terrains of some people are more fragile, and thus more sensitive, than others. But while it might seem obvious that new forms of pathology are appearing, such as those in Japan, nevertheless the notion that these really are new psychopathologies has been challenged by many psychiatrists,[31] on the grounds that they are, in fact, sociopathologies – that is, questions of political economy.

In addition, psychopathological fragility, as a flaw affecting the psyche, is very often, if not always, a source – through compensatory processes that are both well known and completely mysterious – of the most singular individuations, and as such the most precious for the life of the spirit, both on a psychic and a collective level. In the first volume, several cases were discussed where disabilities turned into sources of artistic genius, such as the paralysed fingers with which Django Reinhardt invented modern guitar, or the case of Joë Bousquet, who became a writer through 'wanting to be his wound', or again, the anti-social characteristics (always seen as perversions) of Baudelaire, Rimbaud, and so many poets, not to mention the various forms of madness of Hölderlin, Nerval, Artaud, Van Gogh, and so on. And the deafness of Thomas Edison can also be added to this list.

The INSERM report, completely ignoring these questions, rests on an exclusively normative and health-based idea of the neurological apparatus and of life, and of human being in general. It seems to take no account of Georges Canguilhem's analysis of the normal and the pathological, and fails to see that it is the articulation between the nervous, technical, and social systems that constitutes the total human fact, that is, the real – which has made it possible to understand, since Leroi-Gourhan, that hominization can be analysed as technogenesis and sociogenesis. It is true that psychoanalysis has itself seriously neglected these dimensions, without which there would be no psychogenesis, a problem I have begun to analyse through the concept of 'general organology'.[32]

The INSERM study does venture, albeit hesitantly, some thoughts on these questions, when it emphasizes that the primary question, in terms of the genesis of pathology, is language, which should always also include, more generally, all circuits of symbolic exchange: 'Poor linguistic development hampers the development of healthy socialization, hinders the quality of communication and fosters the expression of defensive reactions in the child.' In the end, the recommendation of this 'panel of experts' is to 'develop new clinical trials, using various treatment combinations and new drugs'.[33]

But to what end? Given that they are probably unable to recommend the use of Ritalin – since that chemical, which is used to 'take care of' American children suffering from 'conduct disorders', has become the subject of an infamous trial – for INSERM it is a matter, on the one hand, of instituting diagnostic techniques with the aim of categorizing and listing children as *a priori* potentially 'subject' to these disorders, and, on the other hand, of proposing that the solution is a chemical straitjacket, that is, a technology of pharmaceutical control, which both opens a new market and avoids the question of sociopathology – which is in fact the only genuine problem.

6. Blaming parents and children is a smokescreen that conceals the question of industrial political economy and leads to the chemical straitjacket

This process of 'culpabilizing' parents and children makes it possible to accuse *them* rather than a society without shame, a society that drives them crazy and destroys them, a society that is no longer loved, and where one no longer loves oneself, where disbelief, miscreance, discredit, cynicism, and stupidity reign. The behavioural disturbances induced by generalized disindividuation are not provoked by genetic *causes*, even if they obviously also possess genetic *bases* – no more or less than some drugs that may be beneficial to an organism but may also, if used excessively, suddenly become toxic. For the genetic bases of irritability are also those of sociability, and are more precisely what Kant called 'unsociable sociability':

> By antagonism, I mean in this context the *unsocial sociability* of men, that is, their tendency to come together in society, coupled, however, with a continual resistance which constantly threatens to break this society up. This propensity is obviously rooted in human

nature. Man has an inclination to *live in society*, since he *feels in this state more than a man* [this is my emphasis], that is, he feels able to develop his natural capacities. But he also has a great tendency to *live as an individual*, to isolate himself [in Japan: *hikikomori*], since he also encounters in himself the unsocial characteristic of wanting to direct everything in accordance with his own ideas. [...] Nature should thus be thanked for fostering social incompatibility, enviously competitive vanity, and insatiable desires for possession or even power. Without these desires, all man's excellent natural capacities would never be roused to develop. Man wishes concord, but nature, knowing better what is good for his species, wishes discord.[34]

This unsociable sociability amounts, therefore, to good *eris*:

> In the same way, trees in a forest, by seeking to deprive each other of air and sunlight, compel each other to find these by upward growth, so that they grow beautiful and straight [...]. All the culture and art which adorn mankind and the finest social order man creates are fruits of his unsociability. For it is compelled by its own nature to discipline itself, and thus, by enforced art, to develop completely the germs which nature implanted.[35]

Unsociable sociability is Kant's way of articulating the psychic and the collective, articulating them as a process of individuation that puts singularity – and the *eris* that it presupposes as competition or emulation, that is, as elevation and transmission – at the core of its dynamic. Now, this is what the standardizations and classifications of this American-inspired mental nosology want to control, in order to reduce it to a behavioural model that would be completely standardized [*normalisable*], that is, calculable.

'Man' – which is the common name for a psychic and collective individuation process – is a being-in-becoming, that is, by default, whose faults are necessary, and are so as his future, that is, as that which constitutes his chances. Even in biological life, as we know, it is the mistakes in the replication of DNA that make possible evolution and the negentropic characteristics of life. Standardizing chemical treatment aims to eliminate these necessary faults: it aims for a flawless process. But such a process would be without desire, for the object of desire is what is lacking [*fait défaut*]. Now, a process without desire is an *irrational* process, which leads to a *demotivated society of chemical straitjackets and electronic bracelets*, or to a *politics of terror*, or, probably, to both at the same time. For beings without desire find their drives loosened and set free, and society is no longer able to contain such beings through repressive measures – nor can it contain the regression that unleashes these drives.

Not only are we able, in *spite* of that genetic irritability that is the molecular basis of unsociable sociability, to do perfectly sociable things, but it is in fact *only* on this basis that we *can* do truly sociable things, that is, individuating, inventive, and civilized things. As for the pathological disturbances from which society does in fact suffer – a society that no longer loves itself and within which stupidity reigns – these are engendered by a system, and the treatment of 'conduct' is one element of this system. This is the system of industrial populism, which has turned attention into a commodity, but a commodity that is losing all value, and which at the same time engenders behaviour that is in fact *socially non-attentive* on the part of disaffected individuals, human wastelands in a general situation of symbolic, spiritual, psychological, intellectual, economic, and political misery.

Disturbed children, fortunately for them, have their faults. But the libido of these children, constituted through these same faults, is diverted from the love objects that are their parents, and from social objects generally – for example, objects of knowledge, or objects of law, insofar as the latter are social concretizations by default of a justice that does not exist – and becomes dangerously impulsive and aggressive, and they suffer terribly from no longer being able to love their parents or their world, just as their parents may no longer be able to love their children: they no longer have the means.

These children then ask for more games consoles, more television, more Coke, more brand-name clothing, or brand-name school supplies, and their parents, subjected to this *pressure to which the social apparatus itself is now totally subjected*, are deprived of their roles as parents. It was in such circumstances that Patricia and Emmanuel Cartier were able to carry out their crime [*passer à l'acte*], but in so doing taking their children with them, thereby affirming – in the same way as do those who, like the London suicide bombers, take themselves to be martyrs – that there is life after death, and that it is better than this life of quiet desperation.

Such circumstances greatly attenuate the culpability of the Cartiers. The question – for any analysis of the conditions in which systems for capturing and harnessing attention, and more generally for inciting consumption, cause 'conduct disorders', including the conditions that led these parents to become infanticidal – is not how guilt should be assigned, but rather to try to think what there is of justice and injustice in the hyper-industrial epoch, and to deduce new political propositions with a future, that is, capable of penetrating the horizon of despair.

Children, adolescents, and parents are seriously unbalanced in their relations, that is, in their being. The passage from the psychic to the collective begins with this relation, which is not therefore secondary but primordial, woven through the primary identification process whereby children, like parents, only are through being in a transductive relation with the family. Currently, this relation is severely disrupted by industrial temporal objects that capture and divert attention, profoundly modifying the play of retention and protention, and above all producing secondary collective retentions that short-circuit the work of transmission between generations, work that is also the only possibility of dialogue, including and even especially in the modes of opposition and provocation. These questions constitute the problematic foundation of what in chapter 2 I referred to as the Antigone complex, and this also means that these questions return to the question of justice, law, and of the hyper-super-egoistic desire of youth, a desire that can turn, if it is abused, into a process of negative sublimation – that is, in some cases, into very dangerous fantasies of martyrdom.

The control of attention and the channelling of primary and secondary identification processes clearly connects the trial of the Cartiers to the trials carried out on children accused of being disruptive and disturbed – for it is indeed a trial they have undergone, and we know that in America such children are treated as sick – children that we sacrifice in this way on the altar of consumption, which is a scandal, a disgrace, and an infamy. To treat them in this way, in a way that responds to the common interests of the pharmaceutical industry, television, and the hypermarkets (such as that hypermarket whose security chief recognized that it was 'sitting on a pressure cooker'), is to make fall upon the little shoulders of these children the decadence of a society intoxicated by its excretions and its products of disassimilation: a society sickened by auto-intoxication, which is a mental destruction and the ruination of 'spirit value'.

The INSERM report, which claims to establish scientifically that these children are pathologically disruptive and attentionally deficient, thus appears for what it is: a trick, concealing the fact that these children are *made* disruptive by a society that has become profoundly pathological, and as such, in fact, inevitably pathogenic. From this perspective, the results of the study are no doubt not false, but the premises through which these results are interpreted certainly are. And the conclusions drawn from these results, recommending chemical treatment of this social malaise and a monitoring process that is clearly about collecting personal data, are catastrophic. They are that much more catastrophic to the extent that they can lead only to a repetition of the kind of thing that has already taken place in the United States with Ritalin.

7.   Lack of attention – or toxicomania as social model

In the lawsuit brought against those pharmaceutical companies that put Ritalin on the market, the issue was already attention deficit and the pathological disorders to which it supposedly leads in children and adolescents: ' "We cannot continue to peddle psychotropic drugs to our children, while at the same time asking them to say no to drugs," declared Andrew Waters, who accuses the American Psychiatric Association of "conspiring to drive American youth to consume tranquillizers." '[36]

What was to be tranquillized was attention deficit disorder, and the tranquillizing pills were composed of methylphenidate, that is, Ritalin, a 'chemical close to amphetamines'. Its range of possible prescription had 'a definition so broad that any disturbed or slightly disruptive child could be included. Result: the number of prescriptions for Ritalin saw a growth rate of 600% between 1989 and 1996.'[37] (A coincidence: Ritalin first entered the market in the

United States in 1989, the same year the Cartiers were married.) The prescription, thus defined, could clearly be applied to all children who, in Europe, America, Japan, and soon China, are becoming more and more disturbed and disruptive, with attention deficits on the psychological level but also the social level, and stupefied by television, video games, and other disorders emerging from hypermarkets and hyper-industrial society, that is, from the industrial populism that is poisoning the world.

How, then, can one not be troubled to see such a 'panel of experts' recommend the monitoring of children who have been identified through 'screening' processes, to be carried out by nurses, schoolteachers, educational specialists, and so on? For, faced with these 'pathologies', which affect not only children but also medical practitioners (for example, Patricia Cartier, who was herself a nurse), as well as the teachers and parents of 'diagnosed' children, and faced with 'parental pathologies' such as consumer credit, addictive consumption, abandoning one's children in front of the television, and so on – in the face of all this, how can we *have confidence* in these institutional structures to 'monitor diagnosed children' in a way that confronts the difficulties faced by these children – in any way other than to make them consume Ritalin, or some more recently authorized equivalent?

For Ritalin was recalled after a trial – but only after it had done serious damage. Let's be clear: we *trusted* Ritalin – and we were wrong. And thus it is worth reflecting on the following:

> [I]n some states, like Virginia, North Carolina or Michigan, between 10 and 15 per cent of school-age children swallow their obedience pills on a daily basis, often after having been reported by their teachers, who bring the parents in for a meeting. The chemical control of teenagers has thus assumed alarming proportions. An Albany, New York couple decided to temporarily interrupt the treatment of their seven year-old son, who had reacted badly. The parents were denounced by social services as 'negligent' and brought before a judge. The judge ordered that the treatment be resumed.[38]

Can we trust INSERM's recommendations for pharmaceutical and institutional measures, or, rather, should we not fight the real problem, namely, the ecological disorder of the spirit in the epoch of cultural and cognitive technologies, monopolized by industrial populism? It would then be necessary to oppose to this an industrial and political economy of the spirit that would be innovative, promising a future, inaugurating a new age of psychic and collective individuation, and, more importantly, that would bring into concrete reality the knowledge society or knowledge capitalism that so many of our leaders or their advisers (such as Denis Kessler) now proclaim as their goal – while simultaneously calling for a 're-enchantment of the world'.

INSERM's recommendations lead to a functional articulation between the psychiatric and the legal spheres, in order to manage the catastrophic devastation that control society causes among parents and children. So, what is all this really about? It is a matter of the relation between *dikè* and *aidos*. To the lack of shame of the symbolic apparatus, which has become diabolical, that is, which contributes to social unravelling, to *diaballein*, and which systematically maintains the regression in which the unleashing of the drives consists, to all this the study recommends adding a repressive system leading to an outright renunciation of the possibility of the super-ego: *the medical profession here internalizes the possibility and the legality of the fact that society is no longer sociable, and that unsociability is no longer able to produce any sociability*, other than by chemically lobotomizing suffering singularities.

Now, the report also recommends that this chemical control, which is a *generalization of the use of addictive systems*, be applied to very young children who have suffered the loss of their parents, that is, the loss of the possibility of primary identification, through which their *imago* is formed. But doing so clearly just establishes a new vicious circle that can result only in a psychopathology leading directly to the catastrophe of *society becoming completely uncontrollable*. Such an absurd spiral is established, in fact, when the children labelled disruptive, or hyperactive and lacking attention, and with conduct disorders, are immediately placed on Ritalin, and where a third of these are

> also prescribed other psychotropic drugs, such as Prozac or anxiolithics, to treat their disorders. Last January [2000], two parents in Ohio sued Ciba Geigy following the death of their eleven-year-old daughter, who had been treated with Ritalin and died of a heart

attack: the autopsy revealed changes to the coronary blood vessels characteristic of cocaine addiction. [...] Children treated with Ritalin are three times as likely as others to become drug addicts.[39]

Toxicomania is the hidden model of a form of social control that has given up on any psychic and collective individuation that believes in the future of unsocial sociability. Faced with these abuses, psychiatrist Peter Breggin, an expert witness in the Dallas trial, stated: 'There is no medical proof of the existence of attention deficit disorder: most children treated with Ritalin exhibit perfectly normal behaviour. [...] [These children] simply need a little attention.'[40]

In other words, the attention deficit comes from society, a society which, nevertheless, blames the children who suffer because of it and to whom it is not attentive, and a society which, at the same time, captures and channels attention onto objects of consumption. The diagnosis is clear. And it is damning.

5

Hope and Politics

Whether we are Christians or atheists, in our universal schizophrenia, *we need reasons to believe in this world.*
                    Gilles Deleuze, *Cinema 2: The Time-Image*

Joy always came after pain.
[...]
Love goes as this water flows
Love goes
Like life is slow
And like Hope is violent
                    Guillaume Apollinaire, 'Le Pont Mirabeau'

There is another world but it is in this one.

                                                        Paul Éluard

1. Emotion and the ways disaffected individuals try to rediscover the feeling of existing

Marketing hype, the imaginary of hyper-consumption, bombardment by television and the media, all hit the suburbs harder than anywhere else: there is virtually nothing there other than screens, giant billboards, and commercial activity zones. Now, the inhabitants of these underprivileged areas are often extremely impoverished, if not totally destitute. Acting out thus seems inevitable – especially considering the stigmatization and ostracism of which these inhabitants are constant victims, and we know the degree to which these accusations are performative, that is, the subjects of unjust accusations are put into a position against which they react, and this reactive behaviour is then used to justify accusations that were initially lies.

Newspapers such as *La Croix* and *Les Échos* have highlighted both the harassing nature of the injunction to consume, which economic poverty makes all the more desirable even as it makes it all the less accessible, and the 'cultural poverty'[1] that prevails in these deserts. What was going on in the riots triggered by a tragic event and by the damaging remarks of a minister – and *La Croix* underscored that the word *riot* in the first place means 'emotion' [*émoi*] – is indicated by Cyril Canetti, psychiatrist at the Fleury-Mérogis prison, who, after interviewing some of these young rioters just after they were incarcerated, concluded that they had committed their crimes *in order to exist*.[2]

Now, Philippe Bilger, lead prosecutor in the trial of Maxime Brunerie, who had attempted to assassinate Jacques Chirac, asked for clemency for the accused on the grounds that he had lost *the feeling of existing*, which was the precise way Richard Durn described his own psychological state immediately before commit-ting the Nanterre massacre. It was also this need for the feeling of existing that the programme *Star Academy* was banking on in order to capture the attention of French children and adolescents. The loss of the feeling of existing is also what afflicts *otaku* and *hikikomori*, and addicted consumers, regardless of whether or not they act out. And this is what destroyed the poor Cartier family. These disaffected individuals all suffer from the same disease, which is not a new psychopathology but a social disorder induced by an obsolete social order – in this case, imposed by an obsolete industrial model, clearly inadequate in relation to the needs of the planet, and in relation to the enormous challenges that must be addressed during the twenty-first century.

The loss of the feeling of existing – which occurs during the psychic and collective disindividuation that results from a dis-identification that is itself engendered by the commodification of attention – gives rise to despair, and may also give rise, for better or worse, to that strength that sometimes accompanies despair, and that is called the 'energy of desperation'. Thinking about despair is possible only from out of a thought of hope – also called *elpis*, another translation of which is 'expectation' [*attente*], and hence which is always a question of attention. And yet, given that according to Emmanuel Carter he wanted to kill his children so they could have a better life after death, it is striking to discover that Nicolas Sarkozy, in *La République, les religions, l'espérance*,[3] defined spirituality, that is, the essence of spirit, as the belief and hope that a better life awaits after death.

The question of expectation is that of hope as well as attention, and as such it is also the question of spirit. The question of spirit, as Sarkozy understands, is also always that of hope and despair. And spirit, like hope, does indeed have an originary relationship with death, because spirit is in the first place what returns, as ghosts return, and as such, what returns from death, and therefore what *exceeds* this death. Does this necessarily mean that the spiritual refers to the hope of a *better life* after death, and that here lies the most profound meaning of spirit or spirituality? Or is this exceeding of death by spirit not rather that which transforms unsociability into sociability, to the strict extent that it organizes the passage from psychic individuation to collective individuation, that is, at the same time, the inscription of psychic secondary retentions into the fund of collective secondary retentions, thereby constituting shared protentional horizons – that is, horizons of hope?

2. Hope and despair

The question of *spirit in its economic and political dimension* is what politicians, more or less, fear and avoid – because, in their great, shared mediocrity, what politicians avoid more than anything is critique, even though it is the very condition of politics. They fear the question of spirit because they are themselves submerged and lost in spiritual misery, of which they are an especially visible and exposed index, if not the most visible and the most exposed. By analysing their discourse we can in a dramatic way gauge the 'decline of spirit value', that is, the increase of disbelief and miscreance, and of the discredit and cynicism which are its consequences. It is by listening to politicians that we most often experience, nowadays, in our industrial democracies, the 'shame of being human': 'And we can feel shame at being human in utterly trivial situations, too: in the face of too great a vulgarization of thinking, in the face of TV entertainment, of a ministerial speech, of "jolly people" gossiping.'[4]

But, conversely, and above all, politicians demonstrate duplicity and a very striking cowardice in relation to the fact that identification is controlled by controlling the perception-consciousness system in which the culture industry consists, a fact they are the first to deny. We of course understand perfectly well the fact that, given that this control is also a matter of controlling public opinion, it is risky for any electoral candidate to antagonize the media, as they are now almost totally dependent on the culture industry – TF1, for example, which acquired a stake in *L'Humanité*. Nevertheless, spiritual misery having become the pivot of all future politics, the political future belongs to those with the courage to struggle against this misery, and who make this struggle their political programme.

In this regard, the discourse of Nicolas Sarkozy, who displays a certain intuition about the significance of spiritual questions in our epoch and about the misery they represent, also attests to the effects of this misery on politicians themselves. It does so in part because Sarkozy's intuitive understanding of this question rests on an erroneous and cursory analysis of the spiritual and religion. More than that, however, his reasoning, like that of all politicians, but perhaps somewhat more explicitly and resolutely than others, essentially consists, on the one hand, in the claim that there is nothing governments can do to struggle against this misery, as if it was simply fate, and, on the other hand, in concealing the fact that the consequence of the symbolic misery induced by the hegemony of the culture industry is the destruction of all shame, and the reign of stupidity and despair.

And Sarkozy's message, defining spirituality as the hope for a better life after death, makes it possible, while speaking of suburban desperation, for him to in fact avoid saying anything whatsoever about what spirit might be *in this world*, and, in particular, to avoid saying anything about the degrading programming policies practised by television broadcasters, policies aimed at the basest drives, which the Catholic faithful (of which he claims to be a member) must fight more than anything. This message makes it possible to conceal the role of industrial populism, which shame-lessly seeks to establish the reign of stupidity in the suburbs, and no doubt elsewhere as well, but probably a little more there than elsewhere, because in the suburbs there is little else.

Citing Alexis de Tocqueville, Sarkozy takes up the idea that religion may be more necessary in a democracy than in a monar-chy: 'Despotism may govern without faith, but liberty cannot. Religion is much more necessary in the republic [...] than in the monarchy [...] and it is more needed in democratic republics than in any others.'[5] But what understanding of religion does this Minister of Religion* hold? Religion, which is in this context practically synonymous with spirituality, is for him essentially hope (that is, expectation): 'My many discussions with victims and their families have led me almost daily to the question of hope and of the meaning of existence. [...] The need for hope is essential to human existence; and [...] what makes religious freedom so important is that it is actually the freedom of hope.'[6]

And such hope, and the belief on which it is founded, is not reducible to trust. This hope is located on another plane than that of the objects of mere trust or confidence, because its object or purpose extends beyond death: its object is the hope for a better life, for a life after death, or, in other words, for an *eternal* life.

3. Eternity and temporality, or *I* and *we*?

Now, this would also mean that questions about life 'here below' are less important than has been said, and than is still believed, in any case compared to spiritual questions, which are the most important, *but which do not concern temporal life*: 'We have overestimated the importance of sociological questions, while

---

* *Translator's note*: At the time of writing, Nicolas Sarkozy was Minister of the Interior (June 2005–March 2007), one of the roles of which was 'Minister of Religion'. He had also served in this post from May 2002 to March 2004. The interview that constituted the basis for the book cited here, *La République, les religions, l'espérance*, was conducted between these two terms, when he was Minister of Finance (March 2004–May 2005).

religion, the spiritual question, has been widely underestimated.
[...] The spiritual question: that is, the question of hope, the
hope of having, after death, a prospect of fulfilment in
eternity.'[7]

The spiritual is what is most important, much more important
than social and sociological questions. But that is not to say it
should be a goal of government: the spiritual is the object of religious rather than public powers, whereas the object of the Republic
is temporal. Hence there is a division of labour to organize between
religions and the Republic, leaving questions of the spirit to those
who understand them:

> The social question is not as essential to the human as is the spiri-
> tual question. [...] Religion deals with the 'essential', that is, with
> the meaning of and the reason for life. Far from threatening the
> Republic, this reflection is useful to it because it is profoundly
> complementary. To religion, the spiritual; to the Republic, the
> temporal.[8]

We can see here that Sarkozy *knows how* to speak about spirit,
and why he is ahead of his rivals on this point: he claims that in
human *existence* there is something that exceeds *subsistence*,
something which lies on another plane, a plane other than that of
existence or subsistence. But he claims at the same time that this
other plane *has no relation to what exists*, that is, to that which
is *in time*, or in other words with that which is '*temporal*'. For
the spiritual is *eternal*. It follows that the Republic deals with life
before death, while religion deals with life after death – with
eternal life, which exceeds death, which does not stop with death:
'The religious is a primary element in that it inscribes within "life"
an element that does not stop with death.'[9]

There is indeed an element that exceeds death, as Kant also
said about that sociability through which the psychic and unsociable individual becomes the common heritage of the universal
we that humanity forms. The problem is, however, that here,
in Sarkozy's discourse, *life after death* is essentially conceived
as *that which has no relation to life in this world*, and the
future that is spirit, that is, spiritual feeling, is only a consolation to overcome the despair that this world inspires, whereas

the Republic can ultimately deal only with social and sociological questions, subordinate questions, emptied of all spirituality
– which also means that what one goes through during one's
lifetime absolutely does not count in relation to the possibility
of hope, or, equally, that temporal life is intrinsically desperate
and hopeless, because it is totally devoid of meaning. Now,
'[m]an is not made to endure despair. [...] Hope in a better
hereafter is an alleviation and a consolation for "living today".
[...] Certainly, there is religious extremism [...]. But can we
condemn those who hope on behalf of a minority driven to
madness by despair and manipulation?'[10]

But what is the meaning here of this word, *'despair'*? Before
getting to that, let us take a look at the way the Minister of
Religion (although he was no longer the minister at the time of
the interview that formed the origin of his book) chooses not to
oppose Catholicism (which he then reveals to be his religion) to
Islam, defining for both the true battle that the faithful must lead:

> The real battle of the Catholic Church in France, today, is not
> against Islam but against the fascination with money, violence, and
> drugs, the loss of meaning in life, the anxiety of many within the
> Catholic community who no longer have hope for the future. The
> challenge is for people to find meaning in their existence.[11]

We know the meaning of this existence is life after death, or what
exceeds death: spirit. But does the question of spirit and religion,
and of what links spirit to religion, in fact amount to the question
of what *exceeds* death *as a life beyond*? Or is it not a completely
different question, a *more interesting and complex* question – the
question, precisely, of psychic individuation insofar as it is always
already collective, that is: insofar as it is what will continue beyond
my death, from the instant of my death, and as the future of my
children, or the children of my family and my friends, of the *we*
that humanity constitutes, as the *we* that is essentially *the unity
of care for our descendants or the descendants of those close to
us, and, step by step, for all our fellow human beings,* so that we
do not hold that attitude expressed colloquially as *'after me, the
deluge'*?[12] This unity of care of a *we* is what forges what I call
consistences, as projections of shared protentions, or in other

words *shared hopes* in *what therefore does not exist*, in fact, but *consists*, while constituting itself through the desire of those who exist, that is, *in the very course of their existence*, and precisely as their *temporality*: as their *individuation*, which is psychic *and* collective to the extent that it proceeds from their *unsociable sociability*.

And as such, hope is more the *perseverance* of a *we* than the eternal life of an *I*. Of course, the meaning of the future is to know what will happen beyond *my* death. But this is not a matter of knowing what will happen *to me* beyond *my* death: to understand spirit this way would be narrow, crude, and backward, as well as selfish, pathologically narcissistic, and ultimately profoundly regressive – it would be an understanding characteristic of the egocentrism specific to the infantile stage of the psyche. The genuine question of the meaning of the future, that is, of spirit, is the question of *knowing what will become of the world after my death* – and such is the question of the future that today makes Catholics, and in fact all of us, apprehensive, whether we believe in heaven or not. That this question continues to *be presented*, historically, and still today, in terms of the representation of the life of the soul after death, in particular in Catholicism, is neither debatable nor insignificant, and still less contemptible. But this just means that it *gives meaning to existence* (as is Sarkozy's wish) only insofar as such a belief constitutes a *guide to living* here below, and especially to living *beyond oneself*, in *attention to others* and in the *succession of generations*. And this opens up the question of *sublimation* as well as of *super-egoization*, that is, also, of idealities.

4. Resurrection in love and religious love as practice

Such is the question of spirit, but here it is a matter of spirit insofar as it involves reason – and as *reason to live*, not to die. That is why, in the end, the Sarkozian definition of the spirit is *desperate*, that is, *absolutely demotivating*, and therefore *irrational* – and contradictory, given that spirit is essentially posed as hope, and this hope seems at bottom to be hopeless. And this is also why it is hardly faithful to the religious spirit of monotheism, which is certainly not reducible to this imagery of eternal life, not to mention that Judaism never cultivated any doctrine of immortality, and in fact neither did primitive Christianity. It was Saint Paul who synthesized Plato's doctrine of the immortal soul with the sacrifice and resurrection of Jesus.

It is clear that the resurrection of Christ opened the possibility of the dogma of eternal life, as Saint John said. But the resurrection, here, refers above all, I believe, to the *return* of the spirit, that is, its resurrection across the *generations, who remember [souviennent] because they retentionalize and protentionalize to the precise extent that they attentionalize*, if I may put it like this, that is: to the extent that they are *attentive*, and attentive precisely through the *repetition of worship* through which they cultivate the *memory of a sacrifice*. Through such worship, Christ comes down [*sous-vient*], that is, returns, and opens the spirituality of the community of the faithful as in effect its shared spirit, and as message of hope. But *this hope, more than life after death, is love*. And love here means that reason which exceeds *ratio*, which is not reducible to calculation, and which is not reducible to temporal life with its petty calculations – by managers and politicians.

Christianity, before it is a doctrine of eternal life and of the imagery that accompanies this dogma, is the religion of a *we* founded on a relation of love, and, as such, it is a form of libidinal economy, like all religions and like all human societies. In this case, it is a libidinal economy that characterizes a psychic and collective individuation process – that is, a relation between the *Is* and the *we* – through regulatory practices essentially consisting in the recollection of the exemplary life of Christ as God of love and sharing. Far from claiming that eternity has no relation to temporal life, such practices, on the contrary, affirm that it is only in this world, and through this way of living, that it is possible to confirm, precisely, the eternity of love and, in this case, the love of God. Now, such worship presupposes practices. And these practices are practised according to a ritual which itself defines a 'calendarity'. And this is why there is, as Nicolas Sarkozy says, 'a universal law of hope for those who practise'.[13]

Now, Sarkozy reiterates that 'the Republic organizes life in its temporal dimension. Religion tries to give it meaning.' But the Minister of Religion also notes that 'weekly practice is

decreasing'.[14] He notes it and he deplores it, after having emphasized (as I have already cited) that in the suburbs, 'within
which every despair is concentrated, it is better that youth have
spiritual hope rather than having their heads filled, as their
only "religion", with violence, drugs, or money. [...] Life is
not goods for immediate consumption.'[15] Yet what he forgets
to mention is that when he was Economics and Finance Minister,
he himself worked to *liberalize the Sunday labour laws*, that
is, he worked *against the practice of Christian worship* – just
as the then Prime Minister, Jean-Pierre Raffarin, felt it necessary to remove the Whit Monday religious holiday.

In other words, thinking about spiritual questions, or what I
prefer to call, more broadly, the question of spirit, has ultimately
not advanced very far – in any case, it is scarcely the object of a
coherent policy for either Sarkozy or his government, in particular
because it is confined to the narrow issue of religion, to which
spirit clearly cannot be reduced: atheists, until further notice, are
not without spirit. They are even called *free spirits*, or *free thinkers*. Spiritual misery has, however, become social suffering, and is
indubitably connected to what is referred to as the 'death of God'.
The Minister of the Interior and Religion knows, despite his own
contradictions, that in speaking this way he may relieve and reas-
sure electors, if only temporarily, beginning with those who have
given up voting, and he claims that spiritual authority is necessary.
But in resurrecting the question of the necessity of a spiritual
authority, which is a very interesting initiative, Sarkozy immediately and carelessly conflates spirit and religious sentiment,
enabling him to avoid asking what spirit is, or what its value might
be, and hence enabling him to propose this need for a spiritual
authority [*pouvoir spirituel*] to the precise extent that it is *opposed*
to temporal power [*pouvoir temporal*].

5. Despair and the politics of mystery as desublimation: the liquidation of the super-ego

Defining spiritual authority as that which organizes a community
united by shared hope in the face of death and in the revelation
of a dogma, spirit becomes, in the politics of the Minister of the
Interior and Religion, the *mystery* that would be the *hope of an*

existence beyond death, and the question of spirit can then be delegated to spiritual communities, leading to the division into different communities of a Republic *where there is no longer anything whatsoever to hope for in this world*, where there is no longer anything whatsoever to *believe in* in this world, at least for the poor (or blank), of which there are many kinds: there is *no longer anything to hope for* other than to project hope onto *another world*. A world that some believe will be populated with virgins.

Such a politics of mystery, in addition to leading to the worst kinds of superstition, is at bottom an organization of disbelief. For belief is first of all belief in the beauty and goodness of the world, and of a world to be built, either by following the example of the life of Jesus, or by complying with the Law, or by adhering to the teachings of Muhammad, or through politics, through the conviction that a liberated life can and must surpass dogma, all dogma, the conviction that there is the strength to exceed what is dead: that there is individuation.

Nicolas Sarkozy acknowledges that the temporal world is desperate, and he argues that religious organizations can bring hope, hope that treats [*soigner*] this despair, that this is the role of such organizations, and that it is not the role of the State. At the same time, he equates the temporal with utility and with the State, which is confined to managing that which is calculable by causing the law to be respected in an essentially repressive way, rather than through any sublimation: *under the pretence of a discourse on the spiritual, he in fact theorizes a politics of desublimation.*

He thus opposes the calculable and the incalculable, which he separates like two impenetrable spheres that must live together on good terms, and by sharing out roles. Hence he enforces to the letter, for example, the traffic law against speeding. He has a clear understanding of the fact that society needs to see this law respected. But to apply the law to the letter is to do so without spirit: it is just cheap confirmation of the spiritual poverty that results from the fact that spirit has passed over to the side of what is not temporal and, beyond that, to the herdish and immediate satisfaction of a collective instinct of conservation, which is called conservatism, and which usually leads to populism. Such a law

must be seen for what it is, namely: created exclusively in order
to keep intact an unjust order.

Nevertheless, by giving signs of 'restoring the authority of the
State' (clearly a classical gesture) through strictly and rigorously
applying the law, while delegating to religious communities that
which, as what raises the spirit, is the only legitimate source of
authority, Sarkozy both intuitively understands that the question
of the super-ego is at the root of the suffering of our epoch,
and that this epoch needs a *new form* of super-egoization. At
the same time, he contributes to the contemporary capitalist
implementation of the liquidation of the super-ego, that is, the
liquidation of all barriers to the circulation and production of
commodities, while claiming that the political future passes
through the affirmation of the 'authority of the State', which
only confirms the translation of this super-egoization into a politics of repression, all the while facilitating and allowing the
unleashing of a televisually conducted regression to the drives.
And the Minister of the Interior and Religion simultaneously
proposes an archaistic and regressive return to spiritual authority
conceived as hope in the beyond, while perpetuating an economic
and social organization that can only increase the reign of despair
on earth, and does so while paying no attention to the message
of social justice which also characterizes Christianity, even
though he nevertheless seems to believe himself to be its faithful
representative.

Now, this is precisely the schema that results in the very bad
ideas that lead the parasuicidal, those who no longer have anything left to lose (and who have no motorbikes or quad bikes with
which they could vent their suicidal fantasies through the kinds
of risk behaviour cultivated by marketing), to act out [*passer à
l'acte*], or, as for example in London, to commit suicide in a way
that takes this for a sublime act, defining itself as sacrifice and
martyrdom. And this is why such discourse, especially when it
comes from the Minister of the Interior, is exceedingly dangerous:
it manipulates the spiritual questions that are so important to
fragile and vulnerable minds, to the point that they believe themselves to be invulnerable to the impotence of the irrational that
hyper-industrial society has become in its current stage – the stage
of spiritual misery, that is, of regression.

For this discourse has nothing to say against degradation, industrial populism, or the liquidation of 'spirit value', starting with that of the religious spirit insofar as it passes through the practices of believers, namely, for Christians, the sacred character of Sunday. This politics of 'spirituality' is in truth entirely conceived in order to accommodate and take advantage of industrial populism, posing this populism as an *unsurpassable* temporal reality: temporal law, which is desperate, but which can change nothing, lies precisely within this very populism, inducing political and economic cynicism, with the result that it is unconcerned with the question of spirit, in the sense that it *does not care*, that is, in the sense that it is perfectly shameless.

6. The loss of psychic and collective individuation is the loss of the 'spirit of capitalism' and leads to 'minoritism'

This is the precise way that capitalism has lost its mind and spirit, renounced it, and delegated it to the sphere of private religion. Capitalism no longer wants to be burdened with the super-ego, or those barriers to free enterprise that the super-ego and religious belief represent – as Max Weber already saw – other than by creating a cheap, trashy religion replete with imagery either of a paradise of eternal life or, for others, of being greeted by virgins. But without the burden of the super-ego, it would be absurd to seek a political belief involving the affirmation that there is the incalculable, which does not exist, but which is necessary to existence, and which must be cultivated in this world, as *belief in this world*, and as the *spirit of reason* bearing *motives* to live which, as *consistences*, are not reducible to the *ratios* of public accounting and managerial control. Since none of this has anything to do with the programme of the Minister of the Interior and Religion, 'communities' are encouraged to content themselves with the role of managing poverty – spiritual poverty. But he is not sure they are prepared for it. And this is indeed suggested by the recent remarks of Benedict XVI about *laïcité* in France:

While condemning violence, Benedict XVI [...] sees two reasons for the crisis: the inability of France to set standards and provide ideals for its youth, and the exhaustion of the French system of integration. The plight of young people worries him: 'It is important to provide young people with social ideals and personal ideals, so that they can hold onto reasons to live and to hope'. [...] Benedict XVI has finally accepted the 'principle of *laïcité* which presupposes a holy distinction between the powers, but does not prevent the Church from taking part in social life, while respecting the competencies of each'.[16]

In other words, the head of the Catholic Church thinks that the State must play its role, and that the Church, which agrees with *laïcité*, can *to this extent* 'take part in social life'.

Spirit, however, according to Nicolas Sarkozy, who presumes to speak in the name of Catholicism, is the very thing that must be abandoned by economics and government. Now, the problem is also, and perhaps firstly, that knowledge, which is also a dimension of spirit – which Sarkozy not only ignores but also denies, given that he claims that the spirit is essentially what exceeds all knowledge,[17] which is not necessarily an unacceptable position,[18] but in this case what this means is that *knowledge is defined as that which denies the spirit*, while the latter *becomes synonymous with mystery* – is what constitutes, as a result of transindividuation, that is, of the formation of collective secondary retentions, and of protentions that take the form of idealities (consistences), the *concrete and social reality of the spirit*, and is that for which capitalism has a great need, in the age of knowledge industries and knowledge societies. (But Jules Ferry already understood this very well, proposing that this is the role of the Republic par excellence.)

Are we, then, to understand that knowledge, for the Minister (who is also a candidate for the highest office of the Republic), must be reduced to mere efficiency, that is, to mere calculation, which, as a new economic power of knowledge, would be totally de-spiritualized, in favour of a notion of spirituality totally reduced to religiosity? This would be to have a very poor idea of the Republic. And to the extent that it is unclear how such a policy would avoid establishing a form of *communautarisme à la* *française*,* as one says here, just as in London, after the attacks of 7 and 21 July 2005, 'the intellectual bedrock permitting Londonistan to be built in the first place retains its relevance. This bedrock is a multiculturalism that regards what differentiates religious and ethnic communities as essential, and that sees what unifies individuals as citizens of the same society – beyond race or faith – as of secondary importance.'[19]

When a priest, an imam, a rabbi, or anyone of faith says that hope lies in another life, and that there lies the essence of spirituality, they do so from within their role as a believer. It seems to me, however, that for a politician to make such remarks, and a politician who is currently responsible for public life, as well as being a candidate to preside over French destiny in these perilous times, and to do so without ever including the message of social justice that is still essential to Catholicism, which he nevertheless claims to represent, can be perceived only as a renunciation – a renunciation that induces profound despair. This message in relation to Hope [*espérance*], far from being a hopeful message [*message d'espoir*], is, on the contrary, despondently resigned.

7. Industrial populism engenders an uncontrollable society haunted by the spirit of martyrdom, and combating this is the absolute political priority

Given that the hyper-power of the rational proves also to be a hyper-vulnerability, in particular when those who believe they have nothing to lose behave irrationally and destructively, and given that such a society, where technological power is only an active power on the basis of confidence in its functioning, and can reverse itself into a hyper-impotence when such confidence disappears, then the mimetic system exploiting industrial

---

* *Translator's note*: *Communautarisme* is a French term the meaning of which is related to both 'multiculturalism' and 'identity politics' (and which in the title of this section was translated, somewhat awkwardly, as 'minoritism'). A useful article on this term in its historical and political context, and in its relation to the term *laïcité*, is David Saunders, '*Anticommunautarisme* and the Government of Religious Difference', *Economy and Society* 37 (2008), pp. 151–71.

populism becomes extremely dangerous, and we await responsible politicians, whoever they are, to draw the consequences. Capturing attention destroys the reasons to wait, and waiting presupposes attention: capturing attention destroys the reasons to expect something from social development. It is thus inevitable that what engenders despair in turn induces uncontrollable behaviour, that is, an uncontrollable society.

During the French riots of November 2005, some rather unusual things took place. According to a report by Élisabeth Lévy, some rioters used their mobile phones to film themselves throwing their incendiary devices, then sold the images to television. Additionally, television crews prepared their equipment at 6 p.m. in areas they considered the most 'explosive', and awaited the commencement of hostilities, so that they could broadcast the images on the 8 o'clock news. This 'waiting' could of course only incite acting out [*passages à l'acte*]. For how much longer will the stupidity industry be permitted to destroy society?

Was it due to such malevolent practices that certain television executives were summoned to the presidential palace? This organization of mimicry was in any case blatant, if not deliberate, and no doubt garnered a large audience, that is, controlled and thus transformed attention into a commodity, at the risk of profoundly distorting it (including within the troubled mind of Alain Finkielkraut),* at the same time that it reinforced the xenophobia

---

* *Translator's note*: The French professor Alain Finkielkraut was interviewed by the Israeli newspaper *Haaretz* in November 2005, and controversially linked the disturbances in France to what he saw as the Muslim identity of the rioters, as well as criticizing the reaction to the riots: 'When an Arab torches a school, it's rebellion. When a white guy does it, it's fascism.' Finkielkraut himself also saw the unrest as related to consumerism, though in a very different way to Stiegler: 'And these people who are destroying schools – what are they really saying? Their message is not a cry for help or a demand for more schools or better schools. It's a desire to eliminate the intermediaries that stand between them and their objects of desire. And what are their objects of desire? Simple: money, designer labels, sometimes girls. And this is something for which our society surely bears responsibility. Because they want everything immediately, and what they want is only the consumer-society ideal. It's what they see on television.' (Available at: *http://www.haaretz.com/misc/article-print-page/what-sort-of-frenchmen-are-they-1.174419?trailingPath=2.169%2C.*)

and simplistic ideas that poison public life in France, and system-atically reinforced the industrial populism that results from these practices.

Sarkozy's reasoning is founded on the opposition of *otium* and *negotium*, that is, on an opposition between spiritual things, understood as belonging to the divine world and hence as being infinite and incalculable par excellence, and worldly things, con-ceived as essentially reducible to calculable commensurabilities without remainder. Now, the reality today is that *otium* has been entirely absorbed into *negotium*, and the culture industries that spread industrial populism are the most striking and problematic realization of this fact. And this is so because, in general, *otium* and *negotium*, which must indeed be distinguished, are far from being opposed and are, on the contrary, always composing: *it is their very composition that forms a world.*

The world is only that which *appears* as *world*, and not as *vile* [*immonde*], *that is, hopeless*, through the circulation of a desire for which the incalculable is not only the divine: it is all that which, not existing, gives to this world its meaning as consistence, and constitutes *the world of idealities, that is, of the spirit*, and, more generally, what opens the process of psycho-social individu-ation to its *intrinsic incompletion*, as Paul Valéry also character-ized it, and *which in fact exceeds death*, even though civilizations are mortal, beginning with the fact that Christian civilization is itself in bad shape.

Such is spirit insofar as it can and must be the object of an industrial political economy – because idealities, like religious ideas, are supported by practices, by supports, *hypomnemata*, which have today become industrial. This also means (and this will be the theme of the fourth volume of *Disbelief and Discredit*) that it is by calculating that we encounter the incalculable, whether divine or temporal – or, more precisely, through the practice of *hypomnemata* as tertiary retention, which puts calculation to work, but which, *as a power of repetition exceeding the drives*, including the death drive, drags out of it not only a difference, but also the experience of a singularity beyond all difference, since it is incomparable.

The tertiary retentions that are *hypomnemata*, then, support *otium* as well as *negotium*. And it is precisely the role of politics, conceived above all as the education of its citizens, to differentiate between *otium* and *negotium* but without opposing them, because such an opposition then leads in fact to the existence of two worlds – that is, to a world where one hand in effect takes what the other has given. In a political society, to struggle against spiritual misery consists in making spirit and its incommensurable value the very heart of political economy, and a political economy inscribed in a general economy that cannot be turned into the economy merely of gift and counter-gift. To delegate this question to religious organizations is, on the contrary, to permanently install this misery, by treating it as a situation against which it is impossible to act, and to indulge in the cultivation of mysteries – and in particular those which lead to negative sublimations among candidates for martyrdom.

By claiming that there is spirit only after death, in an afterlife, because temporal things cannot be spiritual, and therefore offer nothing *for the spirit*, Nicolas Sarkozy confirms secular despair, and that we can do nothing other than pursue a politics of the restoration of authority which – given that it is not supported by the authority of the spirit, that is, consistences – could lead only to authoritarianism, if not to a politics of terror. Such discourse is unfortunately very clear, and can engender only the proliferation of irrational and uncontrollable behaviour, the renunciation of any reason for hope in this world, inevitably inciting the worship of fantasies of sacrifice and a *spirit of martyrdom* that negatively (but irresistibly) sublimates the general suicidal tendency.

8.   Spirit, super-ego, and politics

The *tendency to sublimate* is in fact irresistible – whether this sublimation is positive or negative. It is irresistible because it constitutes the primary goal of all individuation precisely insofar as it is always already both psychic *and* collective, except when it becomes a process of disindividuation.

We are attempting to think the *we* in terms not only of psychic and collective individuation processes, but also of technical individuation processes – tertiary retentions and the *hypomnemata* in which they consist when societies reach the stage of being civilizations submitted to this regime of individuation. The advent of the system of hyper-power, which is also both hyper-vulnerable and hyper-impotent, occurs when, in the process of psychic, collective, and technical individuation, technics, having become technology, then becomes control technology, that is, adopts new forms of *hypomnemata* hegemonically submitted to the imperatives of a hyper-industrial service society. These are the imperatives of capturing attention and controlling behaviour, eliminating *savoir-faire* and *savoir-vivre* in favour of instruction manuals and procedures conceived by marketing to accelerate the adoption of the products of technological (and ever more 'gadgetized') innovation, resulting in an immense process of psychic and collective disindividuation. This disindividuation process is what, in *The Decadence of Industrial Democracies*, I referred to as generalized proletarianization, and it is what leads to the loss of the feeling of existing. That is to say, to despair. This is the context in which spiritual misery is produced, which in turn leads to the tendency towards negative sublimation in a hyper-vulnerable technological system. Such a situation is manifestly explosive.

Powerlessness to combat hyper-vulnerability is the consequence of the irrationality which itself results from demotivation, where those who have lost all reason to hope ruin the trust of those who would otherwise still possess it. Even more seriously, this demotivation is not only a feeling that demotivates individuals, but a *non-motivation* of the world and of the course of things, which become nothing more than disorder and chaos – leading in the end to the conclusion that *existence is completely absurd*. The challenge of any process of psychic, collective, and technical (or technological) individuation is to *constitute its motive, that is, its desire*. This is neither purely psychic nor merely social. And hence it is capable – since imagination is for Valéry the spiritual faculty par excellence, which Kant called transcendental, and which in Deleuze stimulates 'transcendental' stupidity[20] – of engendering a god, or God, but also the triangle, or any ideality, and indeed any sublimity, in particular that sublimating activity par excellence that is artistic labour. And thus, for Nietzsche, only art can penetrate beyond nihilism: 'We possess *art* lest we *perish of the truth*.'[21] For art is what trans-forms and trans-values the groundless [*l'immotivé*] into motives – into motives to live and to love, into motives of desire. The groundlessness of language, for example, is what poetry makes into its sublime motive:

sublimation is always some kind of trans-formation of lead into gold. Some may say that art, too, is in fact no longer an object of love.[22] My response to this (in a forthcoming book) will be that this state of fact, which is extremely important, and a fabulous enigma, is also the fact of the domination of the model of consumption over what, as a result, are no longer called works of art or of spirit, but 'culture', which for more than two decades has commanded less than one per cent of the federal budget. A lack of ambition.

No process of psychic, collective, and technical individuation is possible without super-ego and sublimation. The possibility of individuation, as the *conjoining* of the psychic, collective, and technical, lies in transindividuation, transindividuation as the constitution of a *we* that desires, and where the *I*s desire singularly and yet with one another and for one another. This is why a politics of the spirit, which projects the necessity of the super-ego onto a plane other than that of repression, is indispensable and can consist only in a politics of sublimation. No society has ever been based on anything other than this *power of putting the One together with the Many* – which is the first and perhaps the only question of philosophy. This is what Nicolas Sarkozy confuses with religion, which is only an epoch and modality of the organization of relations between the One and the Many. This confusion is the very spiritual misery of our age, a miserable confusion that Benedict XVI himself, who praises the benefits of *laïcité*, wants to avoid.

The discourse of Nicolas Sarkozy, however, is simply the political and economic claim that follows logically from the liquidation of the super-ego and from its relegation to the side of the mystical and other supplements of the soul – necessary for the peace of the soul, but not till later, in the kingdom of Heaven. In the meantime, this discourse, which I fear actually promises nothing other than war and the loss of the spirit of capitalism, is premised on a profound misunderstanding of the question of the super-ego, of the question of the One and the Many, as well as the question of sublimation, and, finally, of the libidinal economy and its place in the general economy, especially in the epoch in which technologies of the spirit constitute the new ecological question.

All that being said, the point is not to be ironic about politicians, nor about what seems to me the great weakness of their discourse, however much they inspire us with shame (which sends us back to *our own* stupidity). For what is *generally* ignored by the theory of the libidinal economy, including by Freudians, is the role of technics,[23] which also means, in our epoch, the role of industry – which Valéry was almost alone, in his time, in trying to think.[24]

Beyond the economic misery that destroys subsistence, or that deprives those who live within this poverty, and beyond the symbolic misery that destroys existences by dis-individuating psychic individuals deprived of their primordial narcissism and of the feeling of existing, there is a spiritual misery that dis-individuates collective and social individuals and destroys the consistences via which they are co-individuated and constituted through the pursuit and cultivation of the motives that form these consistences as objects of desire for that which does not exist. Struggling against this situation presupposes thinking the role of hypomnesic tertiary retention – that is, of technics – in the constitution not only of these consistences, but also of desire itself, insofar as it is the originarily conjunctive *'and'* of psychic, collective, *and* technical individuation.

The new forms of *hypomnemata* are, today, entirely in the hands of industrial populism, and youth is not only a prime target of marketing but also a group that is particularly sensitive to the power of these hypomnesic forms. Only a politics of spirit proper to these new forms is capable of constituting a motive and a cause for youth – because only practices of *hypomnemata*, and social organizations dedicated to such practices, have ever, since the dawn of time, been capable of constituting a 'spirituality'. A cause for young people is not a supplement of the soul; it is the very future of a society, of a civilization, a culture, and must be worshipped [*faire l'objet de cultes*]. Young people of the twenty-first century have a right to something other than to be policed: they have a right to a future, and to a future that is terrestrial but nevertheless spiritual, that is, elevated.

Youth, its causes, and its elevation are themes which, in the epoch of the lost spirit of capitalism and uncontrollable societies, demand that the question of the super-ego be revisited, a theme that was discussed so much around 1968, that year of 'youth uprising', and of which today's still very crude thinking has opened the door to veritable sociopolitical collapses. We have fought against the super-ego as we have fought against capitalism, and in the belief that this *was* fighting capitalism. Today it is more a matter of saving capitalism from its self-destruction than of fighting against it, although capitalism will nevertheless eventually disappear, to be replaced by a new economic organization: capitalism is only one historical form taken by civilization, and a recent one at that. The super-ego is, by contrast, the condition of *all* individuation, an essential mechanism of the conjoining of psychic, collective, and technical individuation, that is, of transindividuation. And the entire drama and difficulty lie in the fact that capitalism, which must be defended against itself, has become precisely the effective and despairing reality of this liquidation of the super-ego that was so sought after by the protesters of 1968 and their doctrinarians.

Capitalism, as an organization of libidinal economy that exploits energy to the point of destroying it, which is a question of the ecology of spirit understood as a sublimated form of libido, is bound to continue hurtling towards the destruction of the super-ego. And 1968 prepared the way for this: this is one of the theses of Luc Boltanski and Ève Chiapello in *The New Spirit of Capitalism*. The paradox – and the immense historical error, which is also and especially a theoretical error – lies in the fact that capitalism, which was identified with the bourgeoisie, had above all been defined by the affirmation of values referring, as moral framework and justification, to a 'sacralized' right to property.

If capital did in fact justify its position through this bourgeois, puritan, and repressive morality, made the super-ego serve familial and patriarchal values, repressed in particular female sexuality, claimed that property is the foundation of all law, all in the name of the love of God, of God the Father, but also of Christ His Son, figure of the God of love, nevertheless *today's* capitalism – which is, moreover, split between industrial capitalism, based on the mastery of technics and technologies, and financial capitalism, which requires virtually no knowledge – organizes the unleashing of the drives at the same time that it legitimizes expropriation and dispossession in a thousand forms. It is now a matter of dispossessing not merely labourers, artisans, workers, peasants, and so on, but the owners of the 'means of production' themselves – which is a new episode in the conflict between capital and labour.

9.   The life of the spirit as transgression: from the suicidal act to the noetic act

Claiming that capitalism has lost its spirit, this book has tried to describe how psychic, symbolic misery becomes spiritual misery, and what this spiritual misery becomes when it is translated onto the collective plane. The challenge of these questions is the reconstitution of a new spirit of capitalism. But this cannot refer to what Luc Boltanski and Ève Chiapello thought they had identified in *The New Spirit of Capitalism* – even if I am greatly indebted to the analyses of this remarkable work, which in particular makes clear how important it is to show the way in which capitalism was profoundly transformed after 1968, by socializing the discourse typical of the age, which nevertheless failed to constitute a 'spirit'. This socialization – which was made possible through the rise of what Boltanski and Chiapello called technologies of 'connectivity', by which they define this new capitalism – led to what I myself refer to as the hyper-industrial epoch.

Spiritual misery, engendered by the most recent becoming of this capitalism, in that it is capitalism without spirit, leads not only to the psychic dis-individuation of producers and consumers, that is, to generalized proletarianization, but also to a process of the loss of collective individuation, that is, to the outright destruction of societies, to their death. As a result, the challenge of implementing an industrial politics of technologies of spirit, which is the motive both for this work and for Ars Industrialis, is nothing less than the challenge of reconstituting collective individuation, and of struggling against the growing risk of war between the tatters of whatever remains of individuation, wars that are sure to come, including civil wars, if we do not bring the decadence of industrial democracies to an end through a genuine politics. Such a politics should begin by ending a situation for which parents, children, and teachers receive so much of the blame even while they continue to be poisoned and intoxicated by this very situation, insofar as they are also consumers.

The challenge is to re-elaborate a politics of individuation capable of reconstituting the conditions of emergence of a super-ego open to critique, that is, a super-ego exposed to sublimation processes that are also inevitably processes of transgression, that is, of acting out, of a passage to the act, but that would not be that suicidal or parasuicidal acting out which leads to negative sublimation, that is, to uncontrollable, irrational, and inevitably catastrophic behaviour in a hyper-industrial society that is also hyper-vulnerable and hyper-impotent. On the contrary, it is a matter of creating a passage to the act of a genuine possibility of sublimation through the reconstitution of the life of the spirit, that is, an industrial but ecological economy of cognitive and affective functions forming a new civilizational model on the basis of a reorientation of our contemporary industrial reality.

This programme will be the subject of the fourth volume of *Disbelief and Discredit,* along with the question of the *otium* of the people. This will require consideration of *otium* in the Roman Empire.[25] As for the third volume, *The Lost Spirit of Capitalism*, it analyses certain problems in relation to 1968, and attempts to go more deeply into the relationship between the super-ego, sub-limation, and capitalism, through a reading of *The New Spirit of Capitalism*, by Boltanski and Chiapello, and of *Eros and Civilization*, by Herbert Marcuse.

Notes

Introduction

1 On this point, see my commentaries in *De la misère symbolique 1. L'époque hyperindustrielle* (Paris: Galilée, 2004), and in *The Decadence of Industrial Democracies* (Cambridge: Polity Press, 2011).

2 Stiegler, *The Decadence of Industrial Democracies*, pp. 62–4 and pp. 103–7.

3 Luc Boltanski and Ève Chiapello, *The New Spirit of Capitalism* (London and New York: Verso, 2005).

4 Bernard Stiegler, *De la misère symbolique 2. La catastrophè du sensible* (Paris: Galilée, 2005), p. 137, and *Technics and Time, 3: Cinematic Time and the Question of Malaise* (Stanford: Stanford University Press, 2011), ch. 3.

5 Bernard Stiegler, Jean-Christophe Bailly, and Denis Guénoun, *Le théâtre, le peuple, la passion* (Besançon: Les Solitaires intempestifs, 2006).

6 See Stiegler, *De la misère symbolique 2*, epigraph to ch. 2.

Chapter 1 Despair and the Impotence of the Rational

1 Dominique Janicaud, *Powers of the Rational: Science, Technology, and the Future of Thought* (Bloomington: Indiana University Press, 1994). I have previously commented on this work in *Technics and Time, 2: Disorientation* (Stanford: Stanford University Press, 2009), pp. 138–40.

2   This notion of 'decency' is clearly always relative.
3   Patrick Artus and Marie-Paule Virard, *Le capitalisme est en train de s'autodétruire* (Paris: La Découverte, 2005).
4   See Bernard Stiegler, *Constituer l'Europe 1. Dans un monde sans vergogne* (Paris: Galilée, 2005), and *Constituer l'Europe 2. Le motif européen* (Paris: Galilée, 2005).
5   On the question of shame in Greek antiquity and today, see Stiegler, *Constituer l'Europe 1.*
6   On the link between *dikè, aidos, prometheia,* and *epimetheia,* see Bernard Stiegler, *Technics and Time, 1: The Fault of Epimetheus* (Stanford: Stanford University Press, 1998), and *Philosopher par accident. Entretiens avec Élie During* (Paris: Galilée, 2004).
7   On the role in political life of what Jean Lauxerois, inspired by Kostas Axelos, translates so well from Aristotle as amicability [*amicalité*] (in *L'amicalité. Éthique à Nicomaque,* books VIII and IX, tr. and postface J. Lauxerois [Paris: À Propos, 2002]), cf. Bernard Stiegler, 'To Love, to Love Me, to Love Us: From September 11 to April 21', in *Acting Out* (Stanford: Stanford University Press, 2009), and Stiegler, *De la misère symbolique 1.*
8   I first began to develop this point in *De la misère symbolique 2.* I return to it in a more fundamental way in *Mécréance et Discrédit 3. L'esprit perdu du capitalisme* (Paris: Galilée 2006), and will do so again in *Technics and Time, 5,* forthcoming.
9   In my earlier work I proposed that human becoming be analysed as a process of co-individuation involving three strands: the psychic individual, the collective individual, and the technical individual. These individuals are all, as well, systems, constituted of organs, the study of which I have called *general organology.* General organology thus also includes the description of the system of physiological organs that forms the living body, a formation that is itself part of what Simondon described as the process of vital individuation. Psychic, social, and technical systems are open and dynamic, and it is in this way that they constitute processes, processes that co-individuate themselves within a global individuation process. Insofar as they are each processes, they each support a temporality, and co-individuation – that is, the articulation of psychic, social, and technical processes within a single global process – is possible to the extent that the organs of which they are systems support the three kinds of retention that constitute time. My elaboration of this argument thus relies on the Husserlian concept of retention.
    The temporality of the psychic system is that of primary retention, which constitutes the passage of present time for a psychic

being, and which trans-forms itself into secondary retention in becoming the past of this psychic being, that is, its lived experience.

The temporality of the social system is that of collective secondary retention, that is, retentions shared by psychic individuals, either because they have lived through co-ordinated primary retentions that have thus become collective secondary retentions (this is, for example, the basic temporal structure of what one calls an event), or else because they have inherited secondary retentions that they have not lived but that have been bequeathed to them through the social system as the heritage of social organizations, and from the common past of which they are the concretions: this is what is called education.

The temporality of the technical system is that of tertiary retention, that is, objectivations of experience in the form of traces, spatializations of lived time, that make possible the reactivation of this spatialized time, that is, its re-temporalization, either through isolated psychic individuals, who are thus able singularly to access a non-lived past, or else through social individuals, that is, through collections of psychic individuals, and it is in this way that all the innumerable cycles and rhythms are constituted through which social organizations are metastabilized, and of which calendarities (articulated with geo-physical systems and with the solar and planetary system) constitute the vectors of synchronization through which hypomnesic systems, that is, writing systems, appear.

Furthermore, the arrangements between these primary, secondary, and tertiary retentional systems – systems that form, stabilized and spatialized through tertiarization, the pre-individual funds of individuation – can be achieved only through the movement of the global individuation process. But the movement of the global individuation process itself presupposes that there are *motives* that induce this movement, for which retentional systems are both the supports and the materials of projection, in articulation with the body and with the vital individuation that it pursues, *bringing its own motives, those vital motives that constitute the drive-based funds of the living beings that we are.*

I call the *motives* of the process of individuation, again in the wake of Husserl, *protentions*, and I propose that vital protention (that is, the drives) constitutes for the process of psycho-social individuation an archi-retentional and archi-protentional fund.

And I add that justice, *dikè*, as a *primordial motive* of a psycho-social individuation that supports the individuation of the technical system, is such a protention, but a motive that exceeds these drive-based archi-protentions and archi-retentions.

Such 'exceeding' is called desire or, again, reason.

10　See Stiegler, *The Decadence of Industrial Democracies*, pp. 50–3.
11　Ibid., pp. 132ff.
12　'Whence things have their coming into being there they must also perish according to necessity; for they must pay a penalty and be judged for their injustice, according to the ordinance of time.' This is Nietzsche's translation, cited by Martin Heidegger in 'Anaximander's Saying', in *Off the Beaten Track* (Cambridge and New York: Cambridge University Press, 2002), p. 242. This fragment, '*kata to kreon; didomai kar auta diken kai tisin allelois tes adikias*', was translated by Heidegger himself in the following way (according to the translation of the text by Wolfgang Brokmeier): '...along the lines of usage; for they let order and reck belong to one another (in the surmounting) of dis-order' (p. 280). The French translation of Heidegger's translation, in *Chemins qui ne mènent nulle part* (Paris: Gallimard, 1962), is: '*tout au long du maintien; ils laissent quant à eux avoir lieu accord donc aussi déférence de l'un pour l'autre (en l'assomption) du discord.*'
13　See Stiegler, *De la misère symbolique 1*, p. 37.
14　On this point, see note 9 above.
15　Stiegler, *The Decadence of Industrial Democracies*, pp. 133–7.
16　See Stiegler, *De la misère symbolique 2*, pp. 61 and 265.
17　Stéphane Mallarmé, 'When My Old Books are Closed on Paphos' Name...', in *Selected Poetry and Prose* (New York: New Directions, 1982), pp. 59–61 (translation modified); cf., my commentary in *Acting Out*, p. 17.
18　The consistence of justice that cannot be reduced to the existence of positive law requires a judge or jury to judge according to the *spirit* of the law and not only according to its *letter*, that is, it requires someone to judge 'according to their soul and conscience'.
19　And the Greeks were aware that this hypostasization, when it blocks the development of the individuation process, engenders internal conflicts in this process and thereby engenders its possible destruction; this is why '*stasis*' is their name for civil war.
20　This will receive more detailed analysis in *Technics and Time, 4*, forthcoming.
21　Such as, in particular, the pathetic statements by Alain Finkielkraut reported in the media following the recent urban riots.

22 It is such a situation that tries to stage so many spectacles that I have described as *ghastly* [*atterrés*] during an address on contemporary dance during the festival 'Montpellier Danse' in July 2005, and on the theatre during two addresses delivered at the festival 'Mettre en scène', in Rennes in 2004 and 2005. The former has been published in *Mises en scène du monde* (Besançon: Les Solitaires intempestifs, 2005), and the latter, organized in collaboration with Jean-Christophe Bailly and Denis Guénoun, in *Le théâtre, le peuple, la passion*.

23 See p. 8 and note 9 above.

24 Dork Zabunyan, 'L'apprentissage de la bêtise', intervention in the seminar 'Deleuze', organized in 2004 by Patrice Maniglier in the École normal supérieure for the Centre international d'étude de la philosophie française contemporaine (CIEPFC).

25 See Jacques Derrida, *The Post Card* (Chicago and London: University of Chicago Press, 1987), pp. 281–2.

26 See Stiegler, *The Decadence of Industrial Democracies*, p. 104.

27 See ibid., pp. 60–1 and 94–6.

28 Luc Boltanski and Ève Chiapello maintain a thesis close to mine on this point, in *The New Spirit of Capitalism*. I will return to this in Volume 3, always maintaining that it concerns less a new spirit of capitalism than the loss of spirit and reason, which is in fact a very new loss, and which is the ruin of this capitalism rather than its renewal.

29 Despite claims to the contrary by Herbert Marcuse, for example in *Eros and Civilization* (London: Sphere, 1969).

30 Understood here in the sense defined by Martin Heidegger in *The Principle of Reason* (Bloomington and Indianapolis: Indiana University Press, 1991).

31 See Jacques Derrida, 'Force of Law: The "Mystical Foundation of Authority" ', in *Acts of Religion* (New York and London: Routledge, 2002).

32 See Stiegler, *The Decadence of Industrial Democracies*, pp. 10–11; *Technics and Time, 1*, pp. 59–60; *Technics and Time, 2*, pp. 60–1; *Technics and Time, 3*, pp. 6–7.

Chapter 2 The Antigone Complex

1 E.R. Dodds, *The Greeks and the Irrational* (Berkeley and London: University of California Press, 1951).

2   Marie Delcourt, *Hephaïstos ou la légende du magicien. Précédé de La magie d'Hephaïstos par André Green* (Paris: Les Belles Lettres, 1982).
3   See Stiegler, *The Decadence of Industrial Democracies,* pp. 74–80, and Michel Foucault, 'Self Writing', in *Ethics: Subjectivity and Truth* (London: Penguin, 1997), p. 207.
4   The geometric point does not exist (it is not in space) but it permits thinking about space. As such, it constitutes space: it consists, and it consists on another plane, the plane of geometry, which belongs to the plane of idealities in general, that is, of what I here call consistences. See Stiegler, *Constituer l'Europe* 2, pp. 27–9.
5   Sigmund Freud, 'On Narcissism: An Introduction', in *The Standard Edition of the Complete Psychological Works*, Vol. 14 (London: Hogarth Press, 1961), pp. 67–102.
6   See Stiegler, *De la misère symbolique* 2, p. 252.
7   See Stiegler, *Acting Out,* pp. 5–7.
8   Such is Rimbaud's 'Song of the Highest Tower': 'Idle Youth / Enslaved to everything / Through sensitivity / I wasted my life. / Ah! Let the time come / When hearts fall in love. / I said to myself: stop, / Let no one see you: / And without the promise / of loftier joys. / Let nothing put you off / Sublime retreat. / I have been patient so long / That I have forgotten everything; / Fears and sufferings / Have left for the skies. / And an unhealthy thirst / Darkens my veins.' (*Arthur Rimbaud, Complete Works, Selected Letters* (Chicago: University of Chicago Press, 1966), p. 185.
9   Hesiod, *Theogony,* 137–8.
10 This is how Sophocles, in *Oedipus in Colonus*, refers to Antigone: she is Oedipus 'walking stick' (1109).
11 Sophocles, *Oedipus Tyrannus,* 910.
12 Paul, Corinthians 1, 13: 7.
13 Émile Zola, *Au Bonheur des Dames (The Ladies' Delight)* (London: Penguin, 2001), p. 5 (translation modified).
14 Rimbaud, 'Eternity', in *Rimbaud, Complete Works, Selected Letters*, p. 189. The end of the poem was made famous in the Jean-Luc Godard film *Pierrot le fou*: 'It has been found again. / What has? – Eternity. / It is the sea gone off / With the sun.'
15 See Stiegler, *The Decadence of Industrial Democracies*, pp. 53–8.
16 In the word 'abandon', 'bandon comes from the crossing of radical ban- (Frankish *bannjan, "banish"), and band- (Frankish *bandjan, "to signal"' (*Le Robert* dictionary). *La mise au ban* could therefore mean to signal [*faire signe*].

17 '[B]efore a child has arrived at definite knowledge of the difference between the sexes, the lack of a penis, it does not distinguish in value between its father and its mother.' Sigmund Freud, *The Ego and the Id*, in *The Standard Edition of the Complete Psychological Works*, Vol. 19, p. 31, n. 1.

18 Sophocles, *Antigone* 456–7.

19 This question was opened in *De la misère symbolique 2*, and it will be one of the principal themes of *Technics and Time, 5*, forthcoming.

20 On these themes, see Stiegler, *De la misère symbolique 2*, in particular ch. 4, 'Le refoulement de Freud'.

21 We, the generation of 1968, regardless of the attitude that any of us may have to these 'events', should apologize to the young people who will have followed us into this epoch that fails to form an epoch, that produces no *epochal* redoublement. We should ask for forgiveness not out of a sense of guilt, because we are not guilty, but from the feeling of this shame which, alone, as experience of stupidity, and firstly of our own stupidity, genuinely gives us cause to think. This shame is that of the *age of carelessness [incurie]* that was also that of our generation after 1968 – and this is not at all to forget or erase what was also the greatness of what still seemed then to constitute an epoch properly speaking, which we call 'the sixties', during which so many beautiful things took place in so many places.

22 See Stiegler, *Constituer l'Europe 1*, and *Technics and Time, 1*.

23 Sophocles, *Antigone*, 878–84.

24 See Stiegler, *Constituer l'Europe 2*, ch. 1, 'Performance, production, démotivation', and my commentary on Jeremy Rifkin's recent book, *The European Dream: How Europe's Vision of the Future is Quietly Eclipsing the American Dream* (Cambridge: Polity, 2004).

25 See pp. 6–7 and 17–18.

26 See p. 59.

Chapter 3   Spiritual Misery and Reasons for Hope

1 I have outlined certain hypotheses in advancing the concepts of stereotypical and traumatypical retention in *De la misère symbolique 2*, ch. 4, 'Le refoulement de Freud'.

2 Freud, *The Ego and the Id*, p. 31 (translation modified).

3 Ibid., p. 29.

4 Ibid., p. 30.

5 Ibid.

6 Jean Laplanche and Jean-Bertrand Pontalis, *The Language of Psychoanalysis* (London: Karnac, 1988), pp. 431–3.

7 On all these questions, see Stiegler, *Mécréance et Discrédit 3*, p. 19.
8 I began the examination of these questions in *De la misère symbolique 2*, especially pp. 197–218.
9 On this point, see Bernard Stiegler, 'Persephone, Oedipus, Epimtheus', *Tekhnema* 3 (1996), pp. 69–112.
10 And I will return to this point in Volume 4, *L'aristocratie à venir* (forthcoming), through a discussion of Heidegger, the goal of which will be to establish the insufficiency of his analysis.
11 On the question of *eris*, see pp. 19–20.
12 Freud, *The Ego and the Id*, pp. 30–1.
13 There was a time, for example, in my youth, when one made 'sacrifices' for one's children, one's parents, one's brothers, and so on, *believing* in the future, and thus in the *necessity* of these 'self-sacrifices'.
14 I am here using the language of the final chapter of *The Decadence of Industrial Democracies* and of *De la misère symbolique 2*.
15 Freud, *The Ego and the Id*, p. 30.
16 See p. 48.
17 This economic crisis, of which Boltanski and Chiapello recall (in *The New Spirit of Capitalism*) that it is an age of unprecedented prosperity for capitalism, is in reality an economic war, and it is now time to call for and campaign for *economic pacifism* at a global level. It is time to prepare and to sign economic peace treaties, against international accords, in particular those of the World Trade Organization, which, on the contrary, organize this war. This war, to which it is not sufficient to oppose anti-globalization theses that fail to raise the question of changing the industrial model, is in the course of destroying the very conditions of the economic world, which in turn leads to military war. Now, the planet obviously must, given the impotence of the irrational that technological hyper-power has become, be prevented from risking a third world war.
18 And without wishing to confound what he describes with suicidal or parasuicidal behaviour, since it concerns a struggle, but nevertheless including it in this reign of despair that will, if it continues, inevitably become *explosive*, I must here quote at length from a novel by François Bon, entitled *Daewoo*:
   'Perhaps this is what it says, fire. I have no idea: fire, it means being together, and the flame that is carried within. It means a weapon.
   'It had been three days and two nights at the factory, for three days and two nights we had this fire. And the people, what things they brought us: crates, old pallets, logs. The people, in order to

say they were with us, those who had to leave in the morning for work would leave us something for the fire. No one asked for money, nor anything else, except our due.

'So they left us firewood, and the strike held.

'It is this too of which fire is a symbol: a sharing [*partage*].

'*Fire, violence, revolt: Cellatex, a result*

'One hundred and fifty-two workers laid off, a harsh conflict.

'For thirteen days, they maintained their pallet-and-old-tyre fire in front of the gate. Shopkeepers brought them pizzas, sausages. In an old caravan, guard duty was organized, camp beds installed and, under a canvas shelter, card-tables.

'And when there was no longer anything to do, on a Sunday, they sequestered two elected officials and a leader for final negotiations: "Peaceful means were insufficient", they said.

'This Sunday, they turned the factory into a booby-trap: bottles of gas for the Fenwicks, and bottles of acetylene, assembled under the vats of carbon disulphide. Manhole covers to drain the rainwater are removed. The factory is connected to the river Meuse by a stream which, even today, has barely regained its colour, although the grass has come back. To prove they were serious, the workers emptied a vat of sulphuric acid: five thousand litres of acid escaped in a few minutes, bubbling and smoking, while the stream took on an orange hue that lasted a long time. Firefighters pumped the acid into a channel between the stream and the Meuse.' François Bon, *Daewoo* (Paris: Fayard, 2004), pp. 138–9.

How can we not think of those images of fire so complacently shown by television channels during November 2005 in France – and of the fact that fire is, in Greek mythology, both the symbol of technics and the power of Zeus stolen by Prometheus?

19 On the perception-consciousness system, see my commentary in *De la misère symbolique* 2, ch. 4, 'Le refoulement de Freud'.

20 The globality here refers to that about which Ilvo Diamenti wrote, in an article entitled 'Si la lointaine Ossétie devient chez-nous' ['If Faraway Ossetia Comes Here'] published by *La Repubblica* on 5 September 2004, after the Beslan massacre: 'Global terrorism, moreover, by definition crosses all boundaries. It erupts into our world (from the Twin Towers to Madrid). It enters into places of conflict in which the West is implicated, at the side of the Enemy (that it represents). And there, at Beslan, in Ossetia and in Chechnya, the new model is revealed that makes it more difficult to re-shuffle the cards – even if they are put in play – to the degree that we are confronted with what is happening. Situating us and, if possible,

distancing us from the horror and the pain. Reassuring us. It is not only that "cognitive" globalization has discouraged this comprehensible necessity. It is that, in recent years, the geography of political cultures and civilizations has changed. After the fall of the Wall, the market, democracy – in a word, the West – extended and deepened their space. This is why, while being present, alarmed, at the Beslan massacre, we cannot avoid the (embarrassing) thought that Ossetia, at the end of communism and Russia, became "Western".' My thanks to Elena Imbergamo, who drew this article to my attention and translated it.

21 'Man is the animal [...] who raises himself above all other animals through his [...] dreams [to which] he tries indefatigably to submit [nature]. I mean that man is incessantly and necessarily opposed to *what is* through caring for *what is not*. [...] Other living things [...] adapt themselves [...] into a state of equilibrium with their surroundings. They are not [...] in the habit of spontaneously upsetting this equilibrium. [...] They do not feel the spur of that *better* which is the enemy of the good, and that commits us to confronting the worst. Man [...] has it in him to become dissatisfied with what used to satisfy him. At every moment he is something besides what he is. He does not form a *closed* system of needs and of the satisfaction of needs. He gains from satisfaction some strange excess of power that ends his contentment. No sooner are his body and his appetite appeased than something stirs in his depths, torments him, enlightens him, commands him, spurs him on, secretly maneuvers him. And this is Spirit, the Mind armed with its inexhaustible questions ... [...] It divides the past from the present, the future from the past, the possible from the real, the image from the fact. It is both what goes ahead and what lags behind; what builds and what destroys; it is both chance and calculation; it is, therefore, both what is not and the instrument of what is not. It is finally, and especially, the mysterious author of those dreams of which I have spoken.' Paul Valéry, 'The European', in *The Collected Works of Paul Valéry, Volume 10: History and Politics* (New York: Bollingen, 1962), pp. 308–9, translation modified. I have commented on this passage in *Technics and Time, 3*, p. 115.

22 Freud, *Civilization and Its Discontents*, in *The Standard Edition of the Complete Psychological Works*, Vol. 21, p. 114.

23 See pp. 6–7 and 17–18.

24 I will return to this theme of knowledge societies in the fourth volume of this work, *L'aristocratie à venir* (forthcoming).

25 Ernest-Antoine Seillière, in Patrick Le Lay, *Les Dirigeants face au changement* (Paris: Les Éditions du Huitième Jour, 1994), pp. 4–7.
26 In ibid., p. 92.
27 See Stiegler, *The Decadence of Industrial Democracies*, p. 40.
28 See Volume 4, to appear, and *Constituer l'Europe 1*, p. 61.
29 See *The Decadence of Industrial Democracies*, pp. 133–4.
30 And it is striking to note, after the riots of November 2005, the degree to which Alain Finkielkraut, author of *La Défaite de la pensée*, apparently never far from the question of 'transcendental stupidity' as the source of all thinking, not only was *incapable* of thinking the current misery of thought, but seemed himself to be drowning in it like none before.
31 On 'transcendental' stupidity, see p. 24.
32 Plato, *Symposium* 204a.
33 Gilles Deleuze, *Cinema 2: The Time-Image* (Minneapolis: University of Minnesota Press, 1989), pp. 171–3.
34 Bernard Stiegler, 'Temps et individuation technique, psychique et collective dans l'oeuvre de Simondon', *Intellectica* 1/2 (1998), pp. 241–56.

Chapter 4 The Disaffected Individual in the Process of Psychic and Collective Disindividuation

1   See Stiegler, *The Decadence of Industrial Democracies*, pp. 56–7.
2   Florence Aubenas, *Libération*, 17 October 2005.
3   Ibid.
4   Édouard Launet, *Libération*, 17 November 2005.
5   Ibid.
6   Nicolas Sarkozy, *La République, les religions, l'espérance* (Paris: Le Cerf, 2004), p. 18.
7   In Stiegler, *The Decadence of Industrial Democracies*, p. 170, n. 37.
8   See Stiegler, *Constituer l'Europe 1*, p. 33.
9   See notably the works of Saadi Lalhou.
10 Claude Lévi-Strauss, interview with Laurent Lemire, *Campus*, France 2, 28 October 2004.
11 Sigmund Freud, *Beyond the Pleasure Principle*, in *The Standard Edition of the Complete Psychological Works*, Vol. 18, pp. 48–9.
12 See Stiegler, *Mécréance et Discrédit 3*, pp. 91–2 and 117. And see Freud, *The Ego and the Id*, pp. 56–7.
13 See Kenji Nishi, 'Comparative Outline of Criminality', paper presented at a doctoral seminar, Komaba Campus, University of Tokyo,

17 December 2005. In Japan, criminals are asked to repent in order to allow victims to join the land of the dead, that is, to not come back and haunt the criminals. Now, the young man who killed a sixty-four-year-old woman responded that he would repent only if he met the ghost of this woman, which means, in other words, that he did not believe in the possibility that this ghost would return to haunt him.

14 As Kenji Nishi explained to me, this word was coined in 1983 by a columnist in order to refer to those who hang around bookstores specializing in comics or at the markets held twice a year, where comic-book fans sell imitation mangas they have drawn themselves. These are the people to whom the word '*otaku*' refers, but the term is not used in everyday life, because it contains a malicious and hostile implication. The word came into more general use at the end of the 1980s, after the serial murder of four children. The perpetrator, Tsutomu Miyazaki, twenty-seven years old at the time, was described by the media as '*otaku*' because of his collection of comics and animation (television reports showed his bedroom piled high with thousands of videocassettes and comics). The term '*hikikomori*', which is the translation of 'social withdrawal', was picked up by the media towards the end of 1990 in the context of general desocialization, especially among the young.

15 I have drawn some of this information from a private conversation with Hidetaka Ishida, professor at the University of Tokyo, during a trip there from 16 to 22 December 2005, and from his lecture entitled 'Malaise in the Information Society', delivered as part of a conference held on 18 December at Komaba.

16 Available at *http://arthesis.pagesperso-orange.fr/*.

17 Ibid.

18 Bruno Birolli, *Le Nouvel Observateur*, 15 June 2000.

19 Ibid.

20 *Vivre et penser comme des porcs* is, it will be recalled, the title of a book by Gilles Châtelet (Paris: Gallimard, 1998).

21 This does not mean that the world has been de-industrialized, but on the contrary that it has become hyper-industrial.

22 See 'Trouble des conduites chez l'enfant et l'adolescent', 22 September 2005, which may be downloaded at *http://www.inserm.fr/*.

23 Le Lay, *Les Dirigeants face au changement*, p. 93.

24 See Barbara Cassin (ed.), *Vocabulaire européen des philosophes* (Paris: Le Seuil/Le Robert, 2004), p. 1338.

25 'Trouble des conduites chez l'enfant et l'adolescent', p. 333.

26 Ibid., p. 378.
27 Ibid., p. 380.
28 'Criminals should be sterilized and feebleminded persons forbidden
    to leave offspring behind them. [...] The emphasis should be laid
    on getting desirable people to breed.' (Theodore Roosevelt, cited
    in Jeremy Rifkin, *The Biotech Century: Harnessing the Gene and
    Remaking the World* [New York: Putnam, 1998], p. 117.) In 1928,
    more than three quarters of American higher education institutions
    taught eugenics. (Gar Allen, cited in ibid., p. 120.) Earnest A.
    Hooton of Harvard taught that the solution to crime is the 'extir-
    pation of the physically, mentally, and morally unfit or (if that
    seems too harsh) their complete segregation in a socially aseptic
    environment'. (Hooton, cited in ibid., p. 121.) In 1908, Alexander
    Graham Bell, in a speech to the American Breeders Association,
    observed: 'We have learned to apply the laws of heredity so as to
    modify and improve our breeds of domestic animals. Can the
    knowledge and experience so gained be available to man, so as to
    enable him to improve the species to which he himself belongs?'
    (Bell, cited in ibid., p. 121.) Indiana 'passed the first sterilization
    law, in 1907. The bill called for mandatory sterilization of con-
    firmed criminals, idiots, imbeciles, and others in state institutions
    when approved by a board of experts. [...] One reformatory super-
    intendent noted that experts were being pressured by the public
    to explain the apparent inability of state institutions to rehabilitate.
    He observed, "The only way in which their criticism can be met
    is by producing data showing that a large majority of these failures
    were due to mental defect on the part of the inmates and not to
    faults in the system of training".' (Rifkin in ibid., p. 122.) In 1914,
    Harry H. Laughlin issued a report to the American Breeders
    Association in which he explained that 10 per cent of the American
    population were 'socially inadequate biological varieties who
    should be segregated from the federal population and sterilized'.
    (Laughlin, cited in ibid., p. 122.) Rifkin continues: 'With demands
    for sterilization mounting, fifteen more states enacted laws between
    1907 and World War I. The extent to which the sterilization mania
    was carried is reflected in a bill introduced in the Missouri legis-
    lature calling for sterilization of those "convicted of murder, rape,
    highway robbery, chicken stealing, bombing, or theft of automo-
    biles". [...] By 1931, thirty states had passed sterilization laws and
    tens of thousands of American citizens had been surgically "fixed".'
    (Ibid., pp. 122–3.)
29 'Trouble des conduites chez l'enfant et l'adolescent', p. 348.

30 An international association for an industrial politics of technolo-
    gies of the spirit: *http://www.arsindustrialis.org.*
31 See, for example, the intervention of Pierre-Henri Castel during the
    seminar 'Trouver de nouvelles armes' that I led at the Collège inter-
    national de philosophie, in collaboration with George Collins, Marc
    Crépon, and Catherine Perret.
32 See Stiegler, *De la misère symbolique* 2, p. 191. And I return to this
    point in *Mécréance et Discrédit 3.*
33 'Trouble des conduites chez l'enfant et l'adolescent', p. 381.
34 Immanuel Kant, 'Idea for a Universal History with a Cosmopolitan
    Purpose', Fourth Proposition, in *Political Writings* (Cambridge:
    Cambridge University Press, 1991), pp. 44–5.
35 Ibid., Fifth Proposition, p. 46.
36 Gilbert Charles, 'Agitation contre la pluie calmante', *L'Express*, 26
    October 2000, available at *http://www.lexpress.fr/actualite/sciences/*
    sante/agitation-contre-une-pilule-calmante_493069.html.
37 Ibid.
38 Ibid.
39 Ibid.
40 Ibid.

Chapter 5   Hope and Politics

 1 *La Croix*, 12–13 November 2005; *Les Échos*, 24 November 2005.
 2 Media review, on France Culture (radio station), 17 November
    2005.
 3 Sarkozy, *La République, les religions, l'espérance,* p. 11.
 4 Gilles Deleuze, *Negotiations* (New York: Columbia University
    Press, 1995), p. 172.
 5 Alexis de Tocqueville, *Democracy in America* (Washington, DC:
    Regnery Gateway, 2003), p. 245; cited by Sarkozy, *La République,*
    les religions, l'espérance, p. 7.
 6 Sarkozy, *La République, les religions, l'espérance,* p. 11.
 7 Ibid., p. 13.
 8 Ibid., p. 14.
 9 Ibid., p. 15.
10 Ibid., p. 35.
11 Ibid., p. 53.
12 My grandmother, Léonie, who was very pious and practising,
    because Sunday had not yet been taken away, my grandmother who
    believed in heaven, believed she would meet up again with my

grandfather. But this does not mean, contrary to everything that underlies Sarkozy's reasoning, that she was 'afraid of dying'. It means, on the contrary, that she *was not afraid* of dying. And if she did not have this fear, it is because she loved my grandfather *for eternity*. The question of Christianity, the true question *that it bequeaths us*, whether we believe in heaven or not, is that of the object of desire, which, insofar as it is an object of love, is an *infinite* object, that is, the object of an infinite *love*, and thus can only be an *eternal* object. This is what weak and narrow minds, small minds (as one says of petty narcissism, or petty nationalism, or the 'narcissism of minor differences'), can never and will never understand.

13 Sarkozy, *La République, les religions, l'espérance*, p. 16.
14 Ibid., p. 20.
15 Ibid., p. 18.
16 Henri Tincq, 'Le pape aux Français: "Remerciez" vos immigrés', *Le Monde*, 20 December 2005.
17 'I am not sure that the important point is the "why", the explanations.' *La République, les religions, l'espérance*, p. 33. 'Man fears death. He does not know what he will meet in eternity. He is condemned to ignorance.' Ibid., p. 41.
18 I have myself explained why it is not possible to *absolutely* know individuation, that is, to know without individuating, in *De la misère symbolique 1*, p. 96.
19 Gilles Kepel, 'Europe's Answer to Londonistan', openDemocracy, 23 August 2005 (available at: *http://www.opendemocracy.net/conflict-terrorism/londonistan_2775.jsp*, translation modified). The original was published in *Le Monde* under the title, 'Fin de Londonistan, fin du communautarisme?' What follows is equally interesting:

'The unique aspect of multiculturalism is not the emphasis on differentiation as such – for every society is differentiated, chiefly by never-ending conflicts among the social groups driving it; only totalitarian utopias appear free from such fissures. The unique aspect is the belief that individuals are determined by an unchanging cultural "essence" that is particular to each "community", and that the political (and indeed legal) establishment must take these essences into account as a priority.

'In Britain, multiculturalism was the product of an implicit social consensus between leftwing working-class movements and the public-school-educated political elite. Their alliance allowed one side to monitor immigrant workers (Pakistanis in particular) and the other to secure their votes, through their religious leaders, at election time. The July bombings have smashed this consensus to smithereens.

'In one sense at least, and in spite of the massive difference in the number of deaths, British society was more deeply traumatised by the two London bombings than Americans were in the aftermath of 9/11. The United States assailants were foreigners; the eight people involved in London were the children of Britain's own multicultural society.

'They were, moreover, deeply religious men who were radicalised as much (if not more) by videocassettes and the internet as by prayers at the mosque. They seem to have had no allegiance to any of the Muslim community leaders co-opted by the political establishment. They reveal a divided social system where entire groups define themselves primarily through the identity of their religious community, but whose leaders cannot prevent young members of these groups seeking to emulate al-Qaida and fight a war against an "impious" society.'

20   For my part, I believe that the *premier stupidity*, which is the condition of existence as experience of the necessary (de)fault [*défaut qu'il faut*] (and let us not forget that Epimetheus is above all *he who does stupid things*), is that there is just *nothing* that is transcendental, *not even this stupidity* (because even stupidity is lacking, that is, is already composed with the *a posteriori*, that is, with synthesis as artifice). This is what small minds believe to be absurd. I do, however, believe in the atranscendental, that is, an experience in default of the transcendental. This question, which I believe to be the most exciting possible in the twenty-first century, at least for those who love philosophy, will be the subject of the final volume of *Technics and Time*.

21   Friedrich Nietzsche, *The Will to Power* (New York: Random House, 1967), § 822, p. 435.

22   And in fact, as Roger Rotmann recently pointed out to me, we often say that contemporary works of art are 'interesting', without indicating whether or not we like them.

23   And what Freudians also ignore is the culture industry. See Freud, *Group Psychology and the Analysis of the Ego* (*The Standard Edition of the Complete Psychological Works*, Vol. 18) and *Civilization and Its Discontents*, which fail to mention the media, and in particular the cinema.

24   Georges Bataille, who, in a certain way, especially in *The Accursed Share*, tried to develop a thought of the economy of the spirit, nevertheless, in a very classical fashion, opposed spirit to technics, as evidenced, for example, by his remarks on *Homo faber* in *Prehistoric Painting: Lascaux; or, The Birth of Art* (Geneva: Skira, 1955).

25 *Otium* was in Rome above all the experience of the warrior during those times when he was on retreat, according to the work of Jean-Marie André (*L'otium dans la vie morale et intellectuelle romaine des origins à l'époque augustéenne* [Paris: PUF, 1966]; I owe acknowledgement of this neglected work to the perspicacity of Ludovic Duhem, to whom I here express my gratitude), and this seems rather similar to the practices of the Buddhist warriors and soldier monks that originated in the stone gardens of Kyoto, and that were supported by Zen meditation, if not *hypomnemata*.

Index